Advancing Campus Efficiencies

Advancing Campus Efficiencies

A Companion for Campus Leaders in the Digital Era

Sally M. Johnstone
Vice President of Academic Affairs, Winona State University
Former Executive Director, WCET

and

 The Cooperative advancing the effective
use of technology in higher education

 ANKER PUBLISHING COMPANY, INC.
Bolton, Massachusetts

Advancing Campus Efficiencies
A Companion for Campus Leaders in the Digital Era

ISBN 978-1-933371-13-9

Composition by Jessica Holland
Cover design by Frederick Schneider / Grafis

Anker Publishing Company, Inc.
563 Main Street
P.O. Box 249
Bolton, MA 01740-0249 USA

www.ankerpub.com

Library of Congress Cataloging-in-Publication Data

Johnstone, Sally (Sally M.)
  Advancing campus efficiencies : a companion for campus leaders in the digital era / Sally M. Johnstone and WCET associates.
      p. cm.
  Includes bibliographical references and index.
  ISBN-13: 978-1-933371-13-9
  1. Education, Higher—Economic aspects. 2. Education, Higher—Cost effectiveness. 3. Universities and colleges—Computer networks. 4. Educational technology. 5. College students—Services for. I. Western Cooperative for Educational Telecommunications. II. Title.

  LC67.6.J64 2006
  378.10285—dc22

                          2006025790

To
Sally's family—Steve & Emma
Pat's husband—Dan
Russ's wife—Laurie
for their constant support

··· Table of Contents

··· About the Authors

Sally M. Johnstone is vice president for academic affairs at Winona State University and former executive director of WCET, the Cooperative advancing the effective use of technology in higher education. In that capacity she worked with institutions, states, and provinces on planning and policies for the integration of technology into the academic structures of higher education institutions and systems. She also leads workshops and gives about a dozen invited addresses each year to higher education organizations throughout the world. Dr. Johnstone has authored dozens of articles, book chapters, and major reports on open and distributed learning; served on the governing boards of both higher education associations and institutions; and currently serves on the editorial boards of several academic journals. She was a faculty member and an academic administrator after earning her Ph.D. in experimental psychology from the University of North Carolina–Chapel Hill.

WCET is a membership organization of 275 members located in more than 45 U.S. states and 7 countries. WCET members are primarily public colleges and universities but also include private institutions, government agencies, and corporations. The WCET staff develops research projects that focus on integrating technology into the teaching and learning processes, consults with higher education institutions, holds professional development conferences for practitioners, and generally supports WCET members in the planning and implementation of e-learning. WCET was founded in 1989 by the Western Interstate Commission for Higher Education (WICHE).

··· Preface

For the last 17 years, it has been my day job to pay attention to what colleges and universities are doing with information and communication technologies (ICTs). In the early years of our organization, WCET, we focused mostly on academic applications of telecommunications technologies—on what was then called "distance learning." After a few years it became apparent that college and university administrators and faculty were using the things we had thought were part of the distance learning tool bag to accomplish goals in many other areas, not just to serve students who did not come to campus.

WCET's work has covered a wide range of topics in the last decade and a half, but all our efforts have been driven by the underlying belief that current technologies, when planned and used properly, can improve the academy for students and for those who serve students. This can be done by making the academic enterprise more efficient while offering students more opportunities to learn in styles and at paces that are more individualized than has ever been possible.

Throughout this book my colleagues and I draw on our experiences, our systematic observations, and the lessons learned as we used technologies or helped plan for the use of technologies across a broad array of higher education settings. Whether we have been evaluating costs of technology applications, examining the quality of web-based academic courses, guiding the planning of new higher education enterprises (public and private), researching and devising best practices, integrating support systems for students, or helping multinational organizations make sense of changing practices, we WCET staff members have always been learning. This book represents our perspective on what you should know to make good decisions about technology for your college or university.

For those readers who want further information about the projects or research mentioned in the following chapters, we have included references at the end of each chapter. Many of these are web sites that can help you explore specific topics.

Instead of trying to tell the stories of others, many of our friends and colleagues agreed to give us their own words. You will find several essays throughout this volume that are the direct experiences or thoughts of the people involved with the project or topic. We have woven an interesting tapestry of ideas that will help you think differently about how your campus uses ICTs and how you will be able to rev up to meet new demands in a time of fewer resources.

Sally M. Johnstone
Executive Director, WCET
April 2006

··· Acknowledgements

The most important contributors to the knowledge shared in this book are WCET's members. Staffers at our member colleges, universities, state agencies, nonprofit organizations, and corporations have always willingly shared the lessons they have learned—good and bad—and that has enabled us to learn from one another.

Support for our projects has come from the U.S. Department of Education's Fund for the Improvement of Postsecondary Education (FIPSE), the Ford Foundation, Andrew W. Mellon Foundation, Lumina Foundation for Education, the William and Flora Hewlett Foundation, and others. It is these organizations' resources that have made it possible for WCET staff to examine and explore many of the topics covered in this book.

Russell Poulin (WCET), Katrina Meyer (Memphis State University), and Patricia Shea (WCET) contributed chapters on work they have been managing for several years.

Others who deserve special thanks are WCET staffers Sherri Artz Gilbert, for all her efforts in pulling the final manuscript together, and Rachel Dammann, for reference checking. We also want to thank Anne Finnigan at WICHE and Melinda Dodd for assisting us with editing.

Our friends and colleagues who contributed thoughtful essays include:

Russ Adkins, Broward County Community College
Marianne Boeke and *Dennis Jones*, National Center for Higher Education Management Systems (NCHEMS)
Gary Brown, Washington State University
Darlene Burnett, Burnett & Associates
George Connick, University of Maine–Augusta
Anita Crawley, Montgomery College
Steve Crow, Higher Learning Commission

Patricia Cuocco and *Steve Daigle*, California State University Office
    of the Chancellor
Michael Goldstein, Dow Lohnes, PLLC
Gerard L. Hanley, MERLOT
Tom Henderson, Central Washington University
Ed Klonoski, Connecticut Distance Learning Consortium
Andrea Latham and *Connie Graunke*, Florida Department of Education
David Longanecker, Western Interstate Commission for Higher Education
Anne H. Moore, Virginia Tech
Virginia Moxley and *Sue Maes*, Kansas State University
Judith Ramaley, Winona State University
Susan Scott, Indiana Higher Education Telecommunication System
Michael Tagawa, Leeward Community College
Candace Thille and *Joel Smith*, Carnegie Mellon University
Ellen Wagner, Adobe Systems
David Wiley, Utah State University
John Witherspoon, WCET Senior Advisor

Finally, I would like to thank Jim Anker for convincing us to write all
this down to share with others.

··· Foreword

This book is purportedly about technology. Indeed, in the preface, Sally Johnstone says that the book represents "our perspective on what you should know to make good decisions about technology." Yet I think that is too modest a claim. There is, to be sure, a great deal of reference to technology in the pages that follow, and much of it will be informative and useful, as the authors hope. But the heart of this volume is a plea for us to fundamentally rethink the enterprise of higher education.

The book begins with an analysis of the rapidly changing context of American higher education, including such issues as expanding student access in the midst of constrained resources, the changing nature of the higher education enterprise, the impact of the global economy, and emerging definitions of what it means to be educated. Constrained resources have become all too apparent as states have reduced their historic commitment to public higher education to levels once considered unimaginable. Less frequently noted are the changing elements within higher education: issues such as the role of faculty, assumptions about what a college degree represents, and questions about the nature of learning itself. In addition the growing integration of the world economy begins to raise challenging questions about the certification and educational needs of a global workforce.

The core problem we confront is not what technology we should use, but how we should restructure higher education institutions to be effective 21st-century organizations. Scalability, cost, and audience demand that we fundamentally reconceptualize our work. Yet the challenge to change higher education is indeed daunting. Tad Perry reminds us that the capacity to resist change is greater than the resources to implement it. Perry's comment is reminiscent of Steve Portch's facetious comment that it is easier to change the course of history than to change a history course.

Early in the book there is a discussion of how to move from an old model of higher education to a new one. The authors assert that if we are fundamentally to change the design of higher education by reducing cost and increasing access, we must do one or more of the following three things: Exchange capital for labor, exchange lower cost capital for higher cost capital, or exchange low-cost labor for high-cost labor. For senior university leaders, that is the kind of core thinking that must be considered. It is not sufficient to find a particular administrative structure or a specific program that has yielded good results and install it on a campus. Those strategies often ignore local context and history and are rarely successful. Instead, campus leaders might be more successful by thinking about broad principles and then encouraging the development of local strategies that reflect those principles.

Several areas of special interest should be noted. The discussion of open educational resources and the growing movement to place more and more content on the web underscores one of the critical features of the emerging model of the 21st-century university or college. While we will continue to emphasize the discovery of new knowledge, there will be less focus on locally generated content in the classroom. Content is now everywhere, available in incredibly sophisticated forms. I suspect that the emerging university or college of the 21st century will focus more on encouraging engagement—spending considerable energy to ensure that students interact with content in increasingly significant ways. The open educational resources movement and open courseware, specifically, will continue to challenge the way that institutions allocate time and resources.

Another useful focus of the book is on student services. WCET pioneered the development of a new conceptual framework for student services, growing out of its work on services for distance education students. The use of benchmarking and the concept of levels of service are particularly useful ideas for campus leaders to consider.

As we think about change one key issue to address continues to be the level of national arrogance and complacency that challenges each of us. The arrogance comes from our past position of leadership in global higher education, and the refrain, even today, despite growing evidence to the contrary, that we in the U.S. are the leaders of higher education in the world. The complacency comes from the fact that demand is still high, admission offices are flooded with applications, and our reputation remains high despite having slipped some in recent years. Yet just below the surface of apparent reputation and demand lies an enormous challenge from institutions in other countries and from millions of Americans demanding access to our schools.

What makes the challenge so complex is that at its heart the changes being advocated are not about changing focus or direction or about adding a set of new initiatives or programs. What makes this era remarkable is the call for a fundamental reconceptualization of the work of faculty. As Johnstone points out, teaching today is still largely a cottage industry, where a single faculty member, whether brand new or with 30 years of experience, designs his or her own courses, delivers the courses, and evaluates the courses—all of which is typically done alone. Recently, professionals in many other fields have changed the nature of their work significantly, relying much more on technology, using skilled paraprofessional support in different ways, working more frequently in teams, and abandoning some tasks that were once common. Far too often higher education's response to changing circumstances has not been to reconceptualize the work, but instead to hire adjunct faculty to do exactly the same thing tenured faculty do, only at a lower salary. The world envisioned by many of the authors of this book assumes a dramatically different way of delivering courses, disaggregating and reassigning teaching functions, and increasing differentiation, collaboration, and innovation. The authors envision support services provided in new and innovative ways, evaluation conducted by another party or agency—in short, a host of radically different procedural and evaluative structures.

The book ends, appropriately, with a futuristic essay by John Witherspoon that looks forward to 2020, a short 14 years from now, describing the full-blown effects of the forces we already see at work. Of course, the essay only describes the outcomes, not the complex struggles and inspired leadership that will be required to achieve that new design.

The work of leadership is left to each of us, as we address these large issues locally. Achieving its goal, this book will be a companion, both comfort and guide, as we undertake that work.

George Mehaffy
Vice President
American Association of State Colleges and Universities

1 ··· The Journey Begins

Sally M. Johnstone

Now don't mistake me. I'm not advising cruelty or brutality with no purpose. My point is that cruelty with purpose is not cruelty—it's efficiency.

—Captain Bligh, Mutiny on the Bounty

Welcome to a volume of new ideas—and some old ones in a new context. We hope they will be useful for you. Throughout this book, we will be introducing a variety of different topics that center on leading a campus community toward better services for students and more efficient ways of offering them. Many of these new ideas incorporate the wise use of information and communication technologies (ICTs). There will be little discussion of specific technologies in the following chapters, but there will be a lot of ideas presented that will help you think about how to use ICTs to your campus's advantage. This book is not about technology, but many of the ideas in this book relate to the use of ICTs in the creative business of higher education.

Everyone agrees that higher education faces some unique challenges in the 21st century. Student populations are changing quickly. There are fewer males than females on most campuses (King, 2000). Students are *digital natives* and are frequently more technologically advanced than many of their instructors and professors, who are struggling to engage their students creatively. In addition, many campuses are trying to attract more first-generation college students.

There are also more nontraditional institutions offering higher education services than ever before. Some of these institutions are nonprofits and some are for-profits, but all have had the luxury of developing popular new educational programs that are supported by a system that has at its core a business model requiring cost efficiency. Many of these institutions offer high-quality learning experiences to their students, but their program base is quite targeted. They tend to offer lower cost, high-demand programs. Few traditional higher education institutions can do that. Instead, the traditional institutions tend to be comprehensive in nature. They offer high-cost courses, like chemistry and biology, that have labs associated with them, as well as the lower cost courses, such as literature seminars.

To get a more in-depth look at how the for-profit institutions differ from our traditional colleges and universities, I asked Michael Goldstein, a higher education attorney in Washington, DC, who represents both types of institutions, to share his insights.

....

Do For-Profit Institutions Have a Competitive Advantage?
Michael B. Goldstein

Much has been written about the presumed competitive advantages of for-profit institutions. After all, while public and independent colleges and universities continue to scramble for resources, investors pour their money into for-profit schools, precisely because they expect a return on their investment. Simply put, well-run for-profit, degree-granting institutions consistently create a substantial surplus of earned revenue over expenses, whereas such an outcome at public and independent institutions would be exceptional. One common explanation is that "for the most part, the prominent for-profits do what they do quite well . . . 'no-frills' education and training in a narrow set of disciplines" (Pusser, 2006). The corollary is that the public and independent sectors are at a significant economic disadvantage due to the broad array of services and activities they are expected to provide.

While not inaccurate, this may be overly simplistic and does a disservice to all three sectors. While it is clearly the case that for-profit institutions do not have to spend large sums on student activities, athletics, or the maintenance of expensive campuses, this differential is often offset by the enormous difference in the amount of money spent on student recruitment. Whereas independent institutions may spend a few percent of revenues on "enrollment management," it is not uncommon for a for-profit institution to dedicate 15%–20% toward recruitment. This commitment of resources to student recruitment has significantly reduced resistance to for-profit institutions in the degree-granting arena. And with a keen eye on the bottom line, one can be confident that such expenditures can be justified by results.

Another key difference between for-profit and non-profit or public institutions lies in the structure of the faculty (Knapp, Kelly-Reid, Whitmore, Levine, Huh, & Broyles, 2006). About 55% of public institution faculty are part-time (a proportion that increases in two-year public institutions), only slightly higher than the proportion in independent schools. About 70% of for-profit institution faculty are part-time. Not only is the proportion of full- to part-time different, but so is the compensation structure: At the four-year degree level, annual salaries of faculty at public and independent institutions average $67,000, while at comparable four-year, for-profit colleges the average is $39,000. Between two-year public and for-profit colleges the differential is comparable: $53,000 versus $30,000, respectively. This is not a case of exploitation: For-profit institutions tend to rely far more heavily on practitioner-faculty; indeed, the largest such institution, the University of Phoenix, prides itself on the fact that its faculty is drawn from persons who are actively employed in the field in which they teach.

The ability of for-profit, degree-granting institutions to tap into a reservoir of persons who are interested in college-level teaching *contemporaneous* with other employment has been coupled with an increasing utilization of instructional technology. This results in a reasonable level of student services and promotes interaction among faculty and students consistent with the relatively heavy use of part-time faculty.

This leads to a final distinction among the sectors that in turn can weigh heavily on the increasing use of instructional technology: the fundamental financial model. The difference is not that one seeks to generate a return for investors (i.e., profit) and one does not. The difference is far more basic: For-profit institutions have the ability to *create* capital. By selling a share of ownership in the corporate entity within which the school is embedded, a for-profit institution can generate cash that can, in turn, be used to fund the working and long-term capital needs of the institution. Instructional technology is capital intensive, whether to acquire hardware or to create courseware, and it is here that for-profit colleges have an inherent advantage. The transition of some of the most successful for-profit institutions from a conventional classroom model to hybrid online/on-the-ground instruction is emblematic of the value of being able to invest heavily in the technology that will support such a transition.

Michael B. Goldstein has headed the higher education practice at the Washington, DC, law firm of Dow Lohnes since 1978. He is deeply involved in the concurrent emergence of technology-mediated learning and the attendant transformation of the postsecondary market. Prior to joining Dow Lohnes, he was an associate vice chancellor and associate professor at the University of Illinois–Chicago.

Michael has succinctly described the major differences between the emerging for-profit higher education industry and our traditional institutional practices. This does not mean that anyone should expect traditional colleges and universities to behave exactly like the for-profit sector. However, some policymakers who have not looked below the surface of how institutions are managed and how that management evolved seem enamored with this new model. In many states and at the federal level policies are being put into place to push colleges and universities to perform differently. In Colorado, students receive vouchers to use for their higher education. In the U.S. Congress bills have been introduced to level the playing field between traditional and for-profit higher education institutions. There are lessons we may be able to learn from this new force in higher education. We cannot ignore it.

All institutional leaders now face the challenge of learning how to be more efficient within our colleges and universities. In sorting this out, however, it is important to remember the goal and mission of higher education in this country. You do not want to throw out the good practices and capabilities with the less efficient ones. In the following essay, David Longanecker paints an interesting picture of why we are where we are and how we might pay attention to efficiencies.

The Top Critical Issues for Higher Education Today
David Longanecker

Most Americans proudly espouse the egalitarian nature of our modern American higher education system. In many respects, however, this perception neither accurately reflects the current reality nor the essential needs of the future.

American higher education began as an elite system, available only to a few. With the advent of the industrial revolution, however, our nation's focus on higher education changed radically. Enhanced by the Morrill Act of 1862, states began to develop a new invention—the American university. The great American university was unique, illustrating the concept that education and research should be conducted in the same institution, with the same faculty, and the idea that the faculties of liberal arts, humanities, sciences, and technical studies could be blended within the same institution. This expansion in the late 19th and early 20th centuries was not devised to advance the American citizenry, but rather to advance the American society and economy. It reflected a meritocratic philosophy

—that the best and brightest citizens should be well educated for the purposes of advancing the nation. It was not until the 1960s, with the advent of the civil rights movement and the Great Society ethos, that higher education began to adopt the egalitarian principle that all Americans who could benefit from higher education should have an equal opportunity to receive such an education. Out of this new egalitarian philosophy came major efforts at the state level, leading to the development in the mid-20th century of another great American invention—the community college—as well as the radical expansion of public higher education at the baccalaureate and graduate levels. At the federal level, this egalitarian spirit was supported by the creation of federal student assistance programs, most notably the Pell Grant. Originally known as the Basic Educational Opportunity Grant program, the Pell Grant was intended to expand financial access to all citizens prepared to benefit from higher education.

Unfortunately, our national egalitarian spirit has never been realized. Gains in advancing equal opportunity have certainly been made. Over the last third of a century, participation rates for academically and financially advantaged and disadvantaged students have increased. Yet great gaps in parity of participation persist and in many cases have increased. While participation rates have increased substantially for all groups, students' success in completing their education has not increased nearly as much, particularly for students who come from educationally or financially disadvantaged backgrounds. Thus, we are far from achieving our egalitarian goals.

The results of this failure in policy and practice within higher education are beginning to take a toll on our nation and our citizens. Because of the radical expansion of higher education in the early 20th century and following World War II, we led the world in all the benefits that accrue from a comparatively well-educated citizenry, such as economic growth, cultural development, and, yes, sports. Over time, however, the rest of the developed (and even developing) world came to understand the value of investing in education, and our comparative advantage began to fade.

We no longer lead the world in this domain. Today, at least five nations exceed the United States in the share of their young adult population that has the equivalent of a higher education degree; another 10 have rates comparable to ours and will likely surpass us within the next decade, given current participation and success trends. While we have prided ourselves on the quality of our broadly diverse set of colleges and universities, serving a wide array of national and individual needs, recent research has raised issues of the overall efficacy of our system. The recently released results of the National Assessment of Adult Literacy demonstrate that a large majority of college graduates in the U.S. are unable to demonstrate proficient levels of literacy, with many being unable to demonstrate even basic levels of literacy (National Center for Higher Education Statistics, 2005).

It is apparent that we have not yet realized our egalitarian goal of providing high-quality postsecondary education to all who can benefit from it. Even if we had achieved this laudable goal, however, it would not be good enough for the future. Egalitarianism simply won't do. We must adopt a new philosophy, an essentialist philosophy—for it will be essential for almost all our citizens to be much better educated if we wish to keep the U.S. competitive in the new "flat" world of the future.

The most critical concern facing higher education today is the impending collision of the two most significant issues: the exceptional increase in demand that we as a nation will and must face if we are to have an educationally competitive economy and society in the future, and the exceptional constraints in finance that could radically constrain the supply of high-quality postsecondary opportunities to meet the increase in demand.

The Western Interstate Commission for Higher Education's 2003 publication *Knocking on the College Door*, which projects high school graduations, indicates that we can expect only a modest 2% to 3% growth in high school graduates nationally over the next decade, all else being equal. Serving that population doesn't sound like a daunting task; however, averages don't capture the extent of the challenge that this demographic growth will present. States vary widely in the circumstances they will face: North Dakota will face a projected decline in high school graduates of 25% over the next decade, while Nevada will face a projected increase of more than 60%. Furthermore, the ethnic composition of these prospective college students will change dramatically. The projected number of white non-Hispanic students will actually decline by more than 10%, and the number of black non-Hispanic students will decline by 5%. In contrast, the Hispanic student population is projected to increase by more than 50%, becoming the largest "minority" population coming out of high school. These simple demographics portend a huge challenge for higher education, because in the past higher education has not served communities of color well. Doing better in the future will require that higher education change the ways in which it does business.

Simple demographics will not be the only force that drives an increase in the demand for higher education. Every state and national leader recognizes that we, as a nation, must successfully educate a larger share of the population at the collegiate level than we have in the past. This will be essential to the future economic and social vitality of the U.S. Yet these increases in participation and success must come on top of the substantial demographic increases in many sectors of our country. In addition, many adults will need to return to higher education to enhance or refresh their work skills in order to contribute productively to the knowledge-based workforce of the future.

 The combination of these three factors—demographics, essential increases in access and success, and lifelong learning requirements—will drive the demand for higher education well beyond current projections and will create a great challenge for our nation.

Can we afford to pay for this increase in demand? The responsibility for paying for higher education is currently shared among the consumers (students and their parents), the states, the federal government, and other benefactors who value education. It is not clear, however, whether government at the state or federal level can or will maintain its historic commitment to financing the public enterprise. Care must be taken not to overstate concerns about public finance, because many of these concerns are based on myth, not reality. On average, public funding for higher education has held relatively stable over the past 30 years. During the recent downturn of the economy, state and federal funding have fallen, but this is not unusual; in virtually every recession in recent history, funding for higher education dropped substantially but recovered fully in subsequent years. And it appears that states are, indeed, increasing the funding for higher education as state budgets recover.

There are three reasons, however, to be concerned that both state and federal budgets might not provide sufficient funding to support the massive increase in demand that is likely to occur in the near future.

First, there has never before been a post-recession era in recent American history where the recovery occurred at the same time as a substantial increase in demand for higher education. In the past, restoring funding for higher education, by and large, meant simply replacing what had been lost; it did not also demand funding substantial new enrollment. Now, however, states face the task of replacing base funding for institutions and funding new enrollment demand, a much more difficult financial challenge.

Second, the hyperinflationary cost structure of higher education will make it difficult to fund. The costs of higher education will exceed the general increase in inflation, as measured by the Consumer Price Index (CPI), because higher education costs are driven largely by the costs of faculty, who, as highly educated and highly skilled workers, command wage increases that exceed the CPI. Wages for skilled workers generally exceed standard measures of inflation by 1%–2% per year. Over the past half century, American higher education contained overall cost increases by growing predominantly in the lowest cost sector of the industry—the community colleges. This produced a mix of services that allowed each sector to grow more rapidly than inflation, and allowed the whole system to grow at a rate closer to inflation. This strategy cannot continue to work for us in the future, however, because the community colleges have become the largest segment of American higher education. The law of averages won't provide the same benefit of future growth in this sector that was provided in the past.

Third, state and federal governments, whether by choice or capacity, are unlikely to have the fiscal resources to enhance their support for higher education commensurate with the increase in demand. Research from the National Center for Higher Education Management Systems (2002) suggests that virtually every state will face a structural budget deficit within the next 10 years. As demand increases for other services funded by states such as elementary/secondary education, healthcare for the poor and elderly, security, and the rebuilding of a degraded transportation infrastructure, funding higher education adequately will remain a challenge. Furthermore, there is an increasing sense among many policymakers that higher education is as much a private as a public good, thus increasing the interest in shifting a greater share of the burden of financing the enterprise from the state to students, the principal beneficiaries. This is compounded by the antitax sentiment that has captured government and the polity at all levels in recent years.

This confluence of factors raises serious questions about whether public funding will be available to support the burgeoning demand for higher education.

It all makes for an interesting scenario for the future of American higher education. Higher education will be more essential for a larger share of the population, yet individually and collectively we may not be able or willing to pay the price for it. The solution to this dilemma lies in part with the higher education community, which must find ways to more efficiently provide a high-quality product and assure its stakeholders that it is doing so. Technology can help significantly in accomplishing this.

The solution lies in part with policymakers, who will need to recognize that public goods require public support. As one of the wealthiest societies in the history of the world, we certainly can afford to pay for this. The question is, will we?

The solution also lies in part with students. These consumers must recognize that they will have to bear a larger share of the burden of financing their education and preparing for it—if they are to receive education's benefits. Through this shared responsibility, American higher education can be stronger, more accessible, and more economically rational than it has ever been. Indeed, this will be necessary for the U.S. if it is to remain a leading economic, cultural, and social power in the world. Failure to accept these shared responsibilities could spell great difficulties, not only for our nation, but for our citizens. It is our choice.

David Longanecker is executive director of the Western Interstate Commission for Higher Education. He has served as the state higher education executive officer in Colorado and Minnesota, and as the assistant secretary for postsecondary education in the Clinton administration.

As David points out, we are moving into a potential crisis mode in higher education. We cannot continue to do things the way we have done them for the last 50 years. In the dozens of campuses with which I have recently worked, one thing is clear: Campus communities are already doing things differently. Students, faculty, and nonacademic staff members have all embraced the technological tools that are enabling them to be better at what they do.

However, we do not always have the policies in place to support the discovery of the best use of these tools. It is difficult to experiment when student ratings drive salary increases, or annual student success rates drive an institution's funding formula. These practices don't encourage individuals to take risks. In addition, few institutional leaders have had the training (or the time to explore all the issues) to know what has worked at other institutions and what has not. As a field, higher education has not done a good job of learning from others' mistakes. And yet we cannot afford to ignore how others have adapted (or failed to adapt) to the new educational circumstances in which we find ourselves.

Technology and Efficiencies in Academics

Let me describe the scope of ICT already present in our institutions. By the 2000–2001 school year, more than 90% of U.S. public colleges and universities had electronically mediated distance learning courses (Waits & Lewis, 2003). In 2005 42% of the students enrolled in online "distance learning" courses in South Dakota were also on-campus students (South Dakota Board of Regents, 2005). Also in 2005 about 9,000 students at Arizona State University took both online and face-to-face classes (Pope, 2006).

Offering students both online and face-to-face courses is becoming fairly common, and students are beginning to expect it. However, it is critical that these activities are managed in a cost-effective manner, or you merely increase your costs without increasing efficiency. Chapter 2 describes some of the ways in which you can assess your costs for various applications of ICTs. In our work with Technology Costing Methodology projects, a few things have become clear (Johnstone & Poulin, 2002).

The most critical variables affecting the costs of using technology in teaching and learning activities all relate to people. The types of people employed for different tasks, and the salary of those individuals, seem to have the greatest impact on cost variations. If technology is just added on, and changes are not made to the way classes are designed and managed, the result is added cost to the entire enterprise.

In a typical academic approach to online classes, a professor may develop all the online materials for a class, manage the class, and assess the students. In other words, the institution's highest priced academic staff member ends up providing technical, logistical, and academic support to students. This is not the most effective use of this staff member's time, nor is it the most efficient strategy for the use of institutional resources. We need to think seriously about how individuals with different pay levels can play an appropriate role in this whole enterprise. Some new models need to be developed (or borrowed and modified from other systems around the world).

When one looks at costs and begins to think about strategic planning for the integration of ICTs into teaching and learning (either on or off campus), a few more things emerge. Serving students with electronically mediated resources involves much more than just putting course materials online. To be effective and efficient, the whole institution must be involved and committed. Good design of courses is critical, but so is good design of support systems. These are not the same services on-campus students need and use regularly; these are the kinds of services that both on- and off-campus students need to be successful in a modern world. Chapter 3 introduces methods that campuses are using to create efficient, high-quality, web-based support services for all students, regardless of location. This sort of change in support for students can have a profound impact on campus activities and on how successful students are in reaching their academic goals in a reasonable time frame.

If we are going to integrate information and communication technologies into our teaching and learning systems, then we need to accept the costs of designing and developing those technologies. To compensate for the associated costs, it makes sense to have course materials and management systems that can be used by a large number of students. There is evidence that we can develop technology-based and managed classes that do increase students' learning at a reasonable cost per student (see http://center.rpi.edu). Not every campus can afford to develop and support good electronic course materials, even though the current student population expects them. That means we need to find ways to share electronic courses among multiple campuses.

Our most common model for multicampus sharing of academic materials is the textbook. We have experience using the same textbook at several campuses, but few faculty members have experience using imported electronic course materials. This implies some real changes in the job descriptions of some faculty members. Chapter 4 addresses some of the issues and management challenges around the changing faculty roles.

Technology and Efficiencies in Management

There is a growing demand by policymakers for greater accountability measures for higher education institutions. Federal and state legislators are questioning quality indices, persistence rates, time to degree, and costs. Regardless of whether these new accountability demands are justified, higher education leaders will have to determine how to meet them.

One of the most difficult parts of responding to accountability requests is finding the right perspective from which to make your arguments. There is not a single or simple way to approach this. Chapter 5 examines the topic of accountability and offers some strategies. It also reviews in some detail how a specific university system created a technological accountability structure that has served it well with its legislative and student constituencies. In addition, it examines how the accrediting community is responding to greater accountability demands.

One productive approach to achieving greater efficiencies is to develop partnerships with other institutions. These partnerships can take many forms. Some campuses are banding together to negotiate better deals with vendors. Others are sharing electronic networks. Still others are sharing academic materials and even whole courses. Finding ways to work with other institutions is likely to become even more critical as finances get tighter. Chapter 6 offers a look at several different types of higher education consortia and the lessons they can offer, such as how to decide whether to join or form particular partnerships, how consortia evolve, and strategies for engaging the campus community in these efforts to help make them successful.

Finally, we will look at emerging practices that are being enabled by the wide availability of ICTs on and outside higher education campuses. Chapter 7 contains a smorgasbord of new ideas, projects, and activities that are already having a positive effect on the way higher education services are managed and delivered and are likely to have an even greater impact in the coming years.

Institutional Leadership Perspective

In the following essay by Judith Ramaley, you can see why a forward-thinking university president believes it is so critical to pay attention to the ways in which information and communication technologies aid campus transformation. She reminds us all that a good campus leader engages the community.

Leadership in a Technology-Rich Environment
Judith A. Ramaley[1]

Much of my first experience with the realities of cyberspace came from conversations with faculty about their early efforts to design courses for the Internet. It was clear from these conversations that when we work in cyberspace we are more exposed, more vulnerable, and less able to retain the veil of superior knowledge and expertise that has given us a sense of identity as scholars. We can, however, deepen our understanding, practice the disciplines that we love so much more authentically, and enjoy new relationships with the learners who entrust themselves to our care (Ramaley, 2001). This is how technology can influence and further the aims of education. It is also how technology can transform how we work together and how we operate our institutions. On the administrative side of the house, until recently the Internet has been used primarily as a large file cabinet and repository for policies and institutional information. The design of a web site may or may not reflect the habits and real spaces of a campus environment, but the screens we design do send powerful messages about us. These static sites do not, however, expose our thinking in the way that more interactive uses of the capabilities of information and communication technology can afford.

In 2000, the talk was about whether this new technology would be effective or whether it was just another educational flash in the pan that would add to everyone's workload. In the years since those early conversations I had with faculty, we have all learned a lot more about cyberspace, and computers and networks are everywhere. We usually take for granted that the technology will work, and we are very annoyed when it goes down. We know a lot more now about the effectiveness of ICT and have explored some new ways of doing things that the technology makes possible. Most of the applications that capture my own attention now are new approaches to communication. We call our personal digital assistants "crackberries," because they occupy so much of our time and attention. Some advanced college and university presidents are keeping blogs or delivering podcasts that offer their own mental landscape to people whom they may never meet in person.

Some ICT applications open up a new world of insights and an extension of our senses. Through advances in computational capacity and the speed of the Internet, we can see into realms that we could never imagine before. Using ICT we can visualize things as small as an atom and as large as a distant galaxy, or detect the earliest "baby portrait" of our universe after the Big Bang.

When cyberspace first opened up, we simply automated our work without rethinking it. As we painstakingly converted our complex, redundant, confusing policies and procedures into electronic form, we soon realized that we could simplify what we did, reduce the unnecessary steps, and remove those extra signatures up and down the line that added no value to our decisions. We could tie information together so that people would not have to fill out the same dreary paperwork over and over again, making mistakes while they corrected other mistakes. The task of converting our processes and forms to electronic versions made us think in new ways about how we operate our campuses. We could use the mapping exercises that came out of the total quality movement to sort ourselves out and integrate our processes. In this way, never again would anyone have to know how our university is organized or how it works in order to interact with us and do business.

Administrators don't necessarily work in cyberspace the way faculty and students do, but the creation of ICT tools can be a vehicle for changing how we all work together. We have moved from systems designed largely around the convenience of our own work to portals and web environments designed from a user's point of view. We have new collaborative tools and ways to integrate services, and are finding ways to manage our intellectual capital and make our implicit knowledge visible and explicit. The technology makes it possible for us to be a true community of learners—not just a lot of people assembled together, each of us learning on his or her own. Authority used to rest in what you knew that others did not know. Now authority is more closely linked to what you set in motion and how you facilitate the learning and work of others. This is true in the classroom, and it is increasingly true in the workings of our campuses. Teaching and leadership are drawing closer together. They require the same skill. They draw on the same values. They depend upon the same deep trust and openness.

As we have begun to change how we work together, the technology has lowered the physical barriers to working together. It has not, however, lowered the social and emotional barriers that we all bring with us. In fact, I have noticed an interesting pattern shaping up in front of me. The faster we work, the more things we juggle, the more messages we receive, and the more time we spend in electronic communication with each other, the more we want real contact, the comfort of talking in the same space and at the same time with another person. Not having a vocabulary for this longing and not even knowing why we feel the way we do, we accuse the administration of not communicating well, of failing to consult with us. We think that only we are out of the loop and that someone else has privileged access to the increasingly scarce resources that make scholarship possible. We think that somebody else surely must be connected.

The sense of trust that comes from personal contact frays and then snaps as we are flooded with more and more information and have less and less time to absorb it. One aspect of the problem is that many of us learn partly by reading something or looking at images, partly by talking with people, and partly by seeing things for ourselves. Web sites and emails only appeal to one of these avenues for gaining understanding. E-communication may convey information, but it is less likely to foster understanding and then trust. Leadership in an age of the Internet is different. We have open access to more and more material, but we long for real contact and for direct involvement. We want to trust our leaders, but all the elements that build trusting relationships seem beyond our grasp.

ICT is affecting who learns, how they learn, what they learn, when they learn, and what they do with what they know. This is not just true for our students. It is also true for the rest of us. In my own university, computers and networks are ubiquitous. Almost everywhere there is either a wireless environment or an abundance of ports. Students sit in our campus center or, in good weather, out in our gazebo or on the lawn with their screens glowing. They instant message; they play interactive games; they visit chat rooms; they email their professors and each other. They are connected to each other like bees in a hive. They are, as some observers say, natives in the land of cyberspace (Prensky, 2001). Faculty and administrators are usually immigrants in this new land. Perhaps even more accurately, a lot of us have waited for the early pioneers to scout out the territory, and now we are traveling with wagonloads of our own mental baggage, much of which we are forced to jettison along the trail until, finally, we arrive in the new place and learn its language and customs.

I can attest from my own experience that the new capacity afforded by the ubiquitous technology on my campus creates new demands on my expertise, my leadership skills, my capacity to communicate and to inspire, and my ability to tell stories and make meaning. This new environment has the same effect on faculty. Many faculty are still wary of e-learning and cyberspace, fearing that posting their intellectual property in the form of modules and "content" will make them superfluous and that somehow they will design themselves out of a job. In fact, they will be more needed than ever as teaching becomes much more than the integration and interpretation of knowledge. As we move beyond the faithful transmission of knowledge as our goal, we are entering a deeper engagement with learning. The Internet can open access to a vast field of stuff, but it can't help anyone make sense of it, absorb it, or put it to good use. The same is true of the tasks of administration. We can build web sites that are very user friendly, but the real role of educators today (and we are all educators now, whatever role we play on a campus) is to make real contact, to engage each other and our students, to make knowledge visible, and to ensure that the process of learning is transparent and a shared experience.

Leadership in a networked environment rich in ICT is changing in exactly the same way that faculty roles are changing. Leaders,
like educators, must engage others, engender trust, make things real,
connect people and ideas, and serve as a witness to the way that a
community of learners can learn differently. Leaders must actually
work together differently themselves and genuinely make a difference. They must think about technology as a way to lower the barriers to this different kind of work. Only energy and imagination
and a deep belief in the value and dignity of others will allow us to
tap the potential carried by the equipment we have. We have more
capacity already than most people know how to use. We need leaders more than ever. As I wrote in 2001, technology is a mirror. What
we see there may surprise us.

*Judith Ramaley is president of Winona State University. She has also
served as the president of Portland State University and the University
of Vermont, as well as the assistant director of the Education and
Human Resources Directorate at the National Science Foundation.*

As mentioned earlier, the issues and ideas in this book are not about
technology, but they are enabled by the appropriate uses of ICTs. Judith
notes many of the issues we are addressing, and she has crystallized the
challenges that all higher education leaders currently face. There are no
simple solutions, but the more you know of what others have tried, the
more likely your campus will successfully adapt to new students, new
financial structures, and new public demands.

Endnote

1) Many of these ideas emerged during a conversation with Dr. Joan Francioni, chair of our Computer Science Department, Dr. Ken Graetz, director of our E-learning Center, and David Gresham, our vice president for technology and CIO. I also benefited from the insights of Professor Dick Bowman. They are not, however, responsible for what I then did with the ideas we generated together.

References

Johnstone, S. M., & Poulin, R. (2002, March/April). So, how much do technologies really cost? *Change, 34*(2), 21–23.

King, J. E. (2000). *Gender equity in higher education: Are male students at a disadvantage?* Washington, DC: American Council on Education.

Knapp, L. G., Kelly-Reid, J. E., Whitmore, R. W., Levine, B., Huh, S., & Broyles, S. G. (2006). *Employees in postsecondary institutions, fall 2004, and salaries of full-time instructional faculty, 2004–05* (NCES 2006–187). Washington, DC: U.S. Department of Education, National Center for Education Statistics.

National Center for Higher Education Statistics. (2005). *A first look at the literacy of America's adults in the 21st century.* Jessup, MD: U.S. Department of Education.

National Center for Higher Education Management Systems. (2002). *Finance: Projected state and local budget surplus (gap) as a percent of revenues— 2013.* Retrieved August 18, 2006, from: http://www.higheredinfo.org /dbrowser/index.php?submeasure=197&year=2013&level=nation& mode=data&state=0

Pope, J. (2006, January 13). *Some students prefer taking classes online.* Retrieved June 28, 2006, from www.usatoday.com/tech/news/2006-01-15-college -online-courses_x.htm

Prensky, M. (2001, September/October). Digital natives, digital immigrants. *On the Horizon, 9*(5), 1–6.

Pusser, B. (2006, Winter). New competition from for-profit education providers. *AGB Priorities, 27*(1), 1–15.

Ramaley, J. A. (2001, Summer). Technology as a mirror. *Liberal Education, 87*(3), 46–53.

South Dakota Board of Regents. (2005). *2004–2005 distance education enrollment report.* Retrieved June 28, 2006, from the South Dakota Board of Regents, Academic Affairs Council web site: www.sdbor.edu /administration/academics/aac/documents/dist_ed_enrollment_Dec05.pdf

Waits, T., & Lewis, L. (2003). *Distance education at degree-granting postsecondary institutions: 2000–2001* (NCES 2003-017). Washington, DC: U.S. Department of Education, National Center for Education Statistics.

Western Interstate Commission for Higher Education. (2003). *Knocking at the college door: Projections of high school graduates by state, income and race/ethnicity* (6th ed.). Boulder, CO: Author.

2 ⋯ Cost Efficiencies: Tools for Meeting Today's Challenges

Katrina A. Meyer and Russell Poulin

At best, most college presidents are running something that is somewhere between a faltering corporation and a hotel.

—*Leo Botstein, President, Bard College, 1977.*

After coauthoring a controversial article on faculty productivity and efficiencies, a researcher was presenting his findings on what higher education could learn from business models to a somewhat doubtful crowd of academics. At one point, a faculty member rose and said, "Education is not the same as making sausages." The researcher simply acknowledged that he was already aware of that fact. He also said that the statement was intended to quash any further inquiry. But academics know that the essence of research is to question basic assumptions and learn from trial and observation.

In compiling this chapter dealing with costs, efficiencies, and educational technologies, we assure you that we, too, understand that education is not the same as making sausages. At the same time, we challenge the traditional wisdom that implementing technologies can only lead to additional costs. This need not be true. By examining the growing amount of research on this topic, we will show you how technology can be used to constrain costs and increase student outcomes. It *can* be done.

The Trio of Challenges and Technology

Your institution is undoubtedly experiencing the same trio of challenges that face other institutions of higher education. The first challenge lies in dealing with the increasing demands from students, parents, and states for more services, more enrollments, more economic development, and more student services. Unfortunately, funding from the usual sources is becoming more constrained, which is our second challenge. State support for higher education has been dropping for decades, even as the public worries about tuition increases and college affordability. As David Longanecker mentioned in the previous chapter, National Center for Higher Education Management Systems (2002) data indicate that by 2013 all 50 states will have a "structural deficit" in their state budgets. In other words, no state will be able to support its existing services with the revenue that it generates from current tax structures.

A third challenge has to do with the increase in competition from new private and proprietary colleges. Michael Goldstein outlines the differences between nonprofit and for-profit institutions in Chapter 1. One sobering set of statistics on the increased reach of these institutions shows that in fall 2004, the University of Phoenix enrolled 48% of all online graduate business students in the U.S. During the same term, they enrolled 40% of all online graduate nursing students and 27% of all online graduate education students (Ruth, 2006). In short, colleges and universities find themselves grappling with increased competition and increased demand, and they are doing so without any extra funds.

Educational technologies—instructional television, online courses, podcasting—have surely contributed to these problems. States and students demand these services of their institutions. They seek more distance learning courses for adults who cannot commute to campus and for on-campus students who work or are worried about graduating on time. These new technologies and their related services place a serious drain on an institutional budget that is already constrained. Meanwhile, private and proprietary colleges have often been leaders in exploiting the advantages of educational technologies. These same technologies are increasingly being used by public institutions to address their financial problems.

Each institution must find its way to address these challenges, and many institutions have successfully done so. Later in this chapter, we discuss how some institutions have handled such challenges, in the hopes that your institution will be inspired to solve its own challenges.

But what can be learned from the institutions that have used technology—and, more specifically, online courses or modules—to address their rising costs and lack of resources? What steps did they take, and what solutions did they find?

The institutions we look at in this chapter began with a mission and a vision that addressed costs. Then they started to examine what was underlying those costs, closely studying and implementing ways to control or improve them. Next, they made changes that improved overall efficiency and enhanced student learning. This chapter summarizes their experiences so that other institutions may duplicate their successes. But first, let us clarify the differences among cost, costing, and improving costs.

Definitions

The confusion surrounding these terms is partly a result of their misuse, which often happens to terms borrowed from the business world. Take the words "efficiency," "effectiveness," "cost-benefit," and "productivity," for example. All of them have specific meanings, and each directs attention to an institution's inputs and outputs, which can be variously defined (though the examples that follow focus on the teaching-learning process).

Inputs refers to all of the costs and functions that contribute to student learning, such as the cost of faculty, technology, and course design. *Outputs* refers to ways of capturing that learning, such as the quantity of courses offered, credit hours earned, and students who graduate.

Cost efficiency captures the relationship between inputs and outputs, focusing primarily on costs. We say something is cost efficient if it decreases (or maintains) the cost of inputs, and/or increases (or maintains) outputs.

Cost effectiveness also captures the relationship between inputs and outputs, but in this case, outputs are characterized by their value or quality (Levin & McEwan, 2001). We say that something is cost effective if it follows the same rules as cost efficiency, but the value or quality of the outputs improves.

Cost-benefit analysis is a very specific type of analysis that requires that costs and benefits be measured in monetary terms (Cukier, 1997). All elements of this analysis must be expressed in dollars.

Productivity is the ratio of outputs to inputs (or, more generally, the ratio of benefits to costs). Productivity can be used as a synonym for cost efficiency and cost effectiveness, which is confusing and imprecise. In contrast to those terms, productivity tends to emphasize increasing outputs with little or no increase in inputs.

Different institutions use these terms differently. If you are interested in improving costs, it is vital to understand and explain the terms' meanings to your various constituencies. You may want to focus on cost efficiency first, and gradually switch your focus to cost effectiveness. Or you may want to improve productivity—but not at the expense of cost effectiveness. In any case, if you wish to be successful in your efforts, integrate these terms into your institutional planning. The next section describes planning and political considerations when examining efficiencies.

Stating Your Mission Relative to Efficiencies

Your institution may have several good reasons for wanting to understand how its dollars are being used. It may need to find ways to cut its budget, reallocate resources to a new or higher priority initiative, or appear more efficient to constituents. It may need to understand costs in order to set a tuition rate or program price in which the costs are covered by those who benefit most. It may need to understand its own costs, so it can uncover inefficiencies or practices that no longer work as well as they once did. It may need to evaluate the costs involved with increased technology use in order to determine how far it wants to go with online learning. And, finally, it may need to know, because knowing is tantamount to being a good manager of its public resources and its future.

STEWARDSHIP

le 2.1

hnology Costing Methodology Categories of Faculty Activities

truction	Curriculum and course design/planning
	Materials development
	Content delivery
	Tutoring/mentoring of students
	Assessment of student learning
ademic Support Services	Information resources
	Access to/use of technology
dent Services	Admissions
	Advising
	Counseling
ministrative Support	Record-keeping
	Budgeting and finance
	Collection of fees
	Facilities

chnology Costing Methodology Lessons Learned
arianne Boeke and Dennis Jones

ale Matters

most all of the TCM test cases revealed face-to-face instruction to
less expensive than technology-based delivery. This was mostly
e to the fact that many of the courses were being offered for the
st time and had very small enrollments. Technology-intensive
urses have higher development costs, and the number of students
nong whom these costs are divided has a considerable impact on

The great influx of educational technologies in the 1980s and 1990s led
many faculty to study the effect of these new tools on student learning.
Thomas L. Russell's (1999) book, *No Significant Difference Phenomenon*,
compiled hundreds of studies that concluded that students performed just
as well (if not better) in a technology-mediated classroom.

Few early studies reviewed costs, because costs were considered irrelevant until it could be demonstrated that technology was an effective part
of the learning process. After years of experimentation, technology budgets began to mushroom, and legislators and institutional administrators
started asking about the cost implications. While their financial management concerns were legitimate, they sometimes imposed unrealistic
or unhelpful expectations on projects.

Take, for example, the case of the Distance Opportunities for
Interpreter Training Center at the University of Northern Colorado.
This center uses distance education to train people in several rural states
to become interpreters for the deaf. The training is cost effective for students of the program, because they get the training they need without
having to move out of state. Deaf students also realize benefits. For
example, the center's work helps them attend local schools. However, it
is difficult to attain cost efficiency for the institution providing the
instruction, because the small number of people seeking its training
(even in the multistate region it serves) does not readily lead to an economy of scale. You would not impose the same cost efficiency criteria on
this program that you would on a high-enrollment program.

This example highlights the importance of determining whose mission is served by an assessment of cost effectiveness and cost efficiency.
The answers may depend on your point of view: A deaf student who
wishes to remain in the community will certainly see things differently
from a school district that is required to meet accessibility requirements,
a state agency that coordinates the provision of interpreters, or an institution that needs to have its external programs pay for themselves.

While you may think that it is an obvious first step to have clearly stat-
ed goals about costs, this is rarely the case. Most educational technology

initiatives begin by focusing on important goals involving student learning or access, and leave cost implications for future study. To incorporate efficiencies in a meaningful way, any expectations must be built into the initiative from the start.

Regardless of your mission, you will need to know and understand your institution's costs to speak in an informed way about its efficiency, effectiveness, or productivity. All of these things depend on cost information, but knowing that information will not necessarily improve these relationships. The next section describes a costing methodology and explains why it is necessary (but not sufficient) for increasing efficiency, effectiveness, and productivity.

Understanding Cost

The Western Cooperative for Educational Telecommunications (WCET) became interested in costing issues after its members said they needed help understanding the pros and cons of different technology-related decisions. In partnership with the National Center for Higher Education Management Systems (NCHEMS), WCET sought and received funding from the U.S. Department of Education's Fund for the Improvement of Postsecondary Education (FIPSE) to develop a new costing methodology. The new method built on an earlier costing approach developed prior to the introduction of technology on college campuses.

The Technology Costing Methodology (TCM; Jones, 2004) is a form of activity-based costing (ABC), which is different from many other costing approaches. It breaks down costs by instruction-related activity (see Table 2.1) rather than by budgetary line items (e.g., faculty salaries) or allocations of existing department- or college-level budgets (Massy, 2003). Here, faculty salaries are directly connected to the various activities faculty perform, rather than being pooled into one group. This methodology is intended to tease out the cost of specific functions. By knowing, for example, the cost of grading exams by hand, we can easily

identify the cost savings of using a course m form this task.

Of course, the cost of acquiring and mainta ment system must also be broken down by th forms, so grading exams is never "free." But made—the numbers crunched—we can onl having faculty members grade exams is truly ing them graded by a course management sy

Activity analysis reflects the evolving institu one course to several people. A technology-i may require a faculty member who teaches i who develops the course materials, and a teac tutoring and grading. Traditionally, one facu these roles for a given class.

TCM's procedures provide a solid framew tion's costs. At the same time, there are nur calculations and estimates that allow you t suit your institution's unique circumstances ing decisions once, then to ensure compara applying them to each subsequent applicati

Twelve states, thirty institutions, three sta tual high school participated in the pilot te main purpose was to refine TCM procedur ing information about educational techn costs. The pilots were overseen by NCHE and research associate Marianne Boeke (a at the time the TCM project was conducte share the lessons they learned.

cost effectiveness. By increasing the number of students, you increase the efficacy of technology-based courses. Therefore, as a strategy, you should first focus attention on very large courses—those where the economies of scale can be most quickly realized.

Planning Saves Time and Money

There is a trade-off between course planning and development costs. Time spent carefully planning and designing a technology-intensive course is more than offset by a reduction in those costs. Finding alternatives to developing your own content improves cost efficiency because content development is what often makes technology-delivered instruction so expensive. Washington State University's in-depth study on this topic is detailed later in this chapter.

Plan for Increased Student Interaction

The use of technology increases the level of faculty and student interaction, so you must either include inexpensive "mentors" (e.g., teaching assistants) into larger courses or incorporate other strategies (e.g., improved student-to-student or student-to-web site interaction) to develop successful online courses.

Account for "Costs Borne by Others"

Institutions often count on shared services with other institutions or with third parties who serve as test proctors. These "free" services can dramatically affect cost comparisons and decisions about the most efficient ways to deliver instruction. And what happens if one day these services are no longer free?

It's the People

The inclusion of technology and other capital costs in cost calculations is not usually the deal breaker. These costs pale in comparison to your people needs in spite of the large sticker prices associated

with capital items. In the end the things that determine comparative costs are: 1) the amount, type, and cost of the human assets
used, and 2) the ways in which these assets are utilized. You need to
ask yourself if you are drawing on the unique talents of different
kinds of employees, taking advantage of the possibilities of differen-
tiated staffing, and allowing expansion and growth to happen in a
responsible way. In the end your key decisions center around people, not technology.

*Marianne Boeke is a research associate with the National Center for
Higher Education Management Systems. Dennis Jones is president of
the National Center for Higher Education Management Systems.*

Piloting the TCM procedures also led to several policy questions
that Jones and Boeke suggest institutions address when considering
cost effectiveness:

- *Do you need to build all of your own content?* High-quality content
  can be very expensive to develop, so consider buying, leasing, or
  borrowing it from others. This option is often overlooked as "not
  invented here" biases take hold, but quality content will become
  more difficult to ignore as it becomes increasingly available.
  Leasing or buying can be quite attractive, especially as publishers
  increase the usefulness of their coursepacks. The League of
  Innovation's Project SAIL (Specialty Asynchronous Industry
  Learning; see www.league.org/league /projects/sail/index.htm) is
  a fine example of an institution leasing or selling entire programs
  to other institutions. What's more, the Massachusetts Institute of
  Technology's OpenCourseWare (see http://ocw.mit.edu) initiative offers the content used in their courses for no charge.

- *Are you planning for obsolescence?* Financial mechanisms must be
  created to allow for an initial investment in technology assets

and the renewal and replacement of these assets. Capital costs should be a factor in all managerial decisions, and should take short- and long-term needs into consideration.

- *Are you rewarding "good" behavior?* It's important to establish financial mechanisms that recognize and reward all collaborating partners.

- *Would a strategic alliance help?* Institutions often make the mistake of thinking that they can be all things to all people. As we discuss in chapter 6, there are times when an alliance can help you share costs or shift your burden to another entity.

- *Can you make trade-offs between personnel and technology?* If educational technologies simply supplement existing instructional practices, your costs will only rise. As we detail in this chapter, efficiencies require the substitution of one activity for another.

You may have noted that neither this chapter nor TCM focuses on the role benefits play in a cost-benefit analysis. Others have analyzed the subject in depth, but some assistance can be found in the *Technology Costing Methodology Casebook* (Boeke, 2004), which includes an analysis by Stephen Ehrmann of the TLT Group. Ehrmann addresses the question of whether benefits should be the same for all beneficiaries and deals with outcomes, value-added propositions, and categories of benefits (and how to assess them).

While you can't make an informed decision about policy or procedure without knowing institutional costs, there are other things to consider when you pursue efficiencies. You need to understand how efficiencies are achieved, what decisions lead to them, and whether those decisions will work for your institution. The next section will describe several principles of efficiency and explain how cost information can be used to assess and prove that efficiency has been achieved.

Improving Costs

Several studies of technology use in higher education have documented that efficiency and/or productivity can be improved (Twigg, 2003b, 2003c). Improvements result from following certain principles that will later be described in detail. But before they can be discussed, the question of how to focus an institution's efficiency efforts must be addressed.

At this stage three important decisions need to be made concerning efficiencies. First, online courses require a radical change in an institution's distribution of costs, because they require higher development costs. It takes several people, including faculty, instructional designers, and library and media personnel, to design a good online course. Second, because of those higher development costs, institutions have to focus on lowering operational costs (i.e., their costs per enrolled student). Third, the online course that will incur these development costs must be chosen carefully.

Four types of courses may be the best candidates for consideration. First, there are 25 courses that generate about half of all student enrollments in community colleges and one-third of all enrollments at four-year institutions (Twigg, 2003b), so they would naturally be a good choice. Second, high-enrollment courses in a curriculum or major could also be candidates for inclusion, as could the third type, problem or gateway courses. These are courses that students need to master, but often fail or drop. Finally, standard, common courses with relatively stable content (which rarely needs to be updated) might be considered. In each case, the cost of developing the courses would be reduced each time they were taught.

In short, institutions need to be more proactive and deliberative about investing in the development of online courses. That doesn't mean that faculty shouldn't put individual courses online, but it does mean that you need to look at how you ultimately use your institutional resources. Faculty members can actually help improve costs, if they understand them—even if it occurs on a smaller scale.

How can your institution become more efficient? Efficiency is the result of three substitutions and economies of scale. The substitutions are *capital for labor, capital for capital, and lower cost labor for higher cost labor.*

First, how do institutions substitute capital for labor and become more cost efficient? Simple. Institutions invest in capital, such as online courses, modules, and grading programs, that enable faculty to spend less time on instruction. This could be a slightly frightening change for faculty members, but their time can be better used to advise students, diagnose learning problems, design new lessons, evaluate and upgrade courses, and focus on specialized instruction for upper division or graduate students. Despite the change, there will still be plenty of work, although the fear the change engenders must be acknowledged.

The following are examples of how institutions have substituted *capital for labor:*

- Pennsylvania State University used computer-mediated instruction to decrease the time teachers spent lecturing (Twigg, 2003b).

- Online modules were used to save faculty time at the University of Central Florida (Twigg, 2003b).

- Brigham Young University implemented multimedia lessons (Waddoups, Hatch, & Butterworth, 2003).

- Online quizzes offered feedback to students at the University of Central Florida (Fisher & Nygren, 2000).

- Online quizzes provided personalized problem sets, quizzes, and exams at Texas A & M University (Fisher & Nygren, 2000).

- Online quizzes helped students at the University of Illinois assess their own progress and identify what they needed to work on (Avran, Ory, Bullock, Burnaska, & Hanson, 1998).

- Online grading and the use of course management systems reduced faculty time spent on recording, calculating, and storing grades; photocopying materials; posting changes; and sending out announcements at the University of Buffalo (Twigg, 2003a).

- Instructional software helped Texas A & M University faculty spend less time lecturing and grading quizzes, and reduced the number of faculty teaching a course on psychology statistics from five to one (Fisher & Nygren, 2000).

- Multimedia lessons and one-on-one meetings with writing teachers helped produce better papers at Brigham Young University, and reduced overall class meeting time and the amount of time faculty spent on courses by 25% (Waddoups, Hatch, & Butterworth, 2003).

Carol Twigg (2003b) created the Program in Course Redesign in 1999 as part of the National Center for Academic Transformation, with support from the Pew Charitable Trusts. As the center's web site (www.then cat.org) explains, from 1999–2004, the staff worked with 30 diverse two- and four-year colleges (in an effort that involved 50,000 students annually) to prove that it is possible to improve student learning and reduce cost in higher education. Through online and computer-mediated instruction, online modules or labs, and the automatic testing and grading of most courseware packages, institutions were able to reduce course delivery costs by an average of 40%, with savings that ranged from 20%–86%—an annual cost savings of more than $3.6 million— while making an impact on more than 50,000 students. The results of the Program in Course Redesign were exceptional: 25 of 30 course redesign projects showed significant increases in student learning, while the other 5 showed learning at levels equivalent to traditional formats. Of the 24 projects that measured retention, 18 reported a noticeable (10%–20%) decrease in drop-failure-withdrawal rates, as well as higher course-completion rates. Other positive outcomes included better student attitudes toward the subject matter and increased student and faculty satisfaction with the new mode of instruction.

Institutions often substitute *capital for capital* when dealing with infrastructure challenges. As enrollment grows and instructional space remains limited, several colleges and universities have gone online to broaden course availability. For example:

- The University of Central Florida saved classroom space by delivering portions of its courses online. Since two or three sections could be held in the same classroom, there was no need to build or rent new space.

- Vanderbilt University used simulation software in sophomore-level electrical engineering and found that students learned as much in the simulated labs as they did in real ones. Campbell, Bourne, Mosterman, Nahvi, Rassai, Brodersen, et al. (2004) concluded that simulation software could "replace some physical labs" (p. 9), which would also lower the cost of lab equipment and supplies.

- The National Small Scale Chemistry Center at Colorado State University (see www.smallscalechemistry.colostate.edu) has developed a low-cost kit that replaces a traditional chemistry lab. It retains learning outcomes, uses safer chemicals, and is 25 to 32 times less expensive.

- Virginia Tech created a virtual math lab, freeing up space so more students could enroll—and succeed—in entry-level math courses (Twigg, 2003b, 2003c).

In each of these cases, online courses or laboratories acted as substitutes for capital space—and in each case, institutional costs were reduced.

With the careful design of online courses, you can substitute *low-cost labor for higher cost faculty.* We're not suggesting you replace faculty with adjuncts, however (as some might fear). Chapter 4 contains a more thorough discussion of how low-cost labor and a lower level of faculty expertise can best be utilized for student learning.

Several institutions have created online modules, virtual labs, computer-mediated exercises, and online quizzes and tests that are so robust that instructional support can be provided by relatively inexpensive assistants. Graduate assistants, teaching assistants, undergraduate peers, and part-time instructional staff can answer technical questions, diagnose simple learning mistakes, and provide help in other ways. For example:

- Rio Salado College used course assistants to answer nonmath-related questions, accounting for 90% of its interactions with students (Twigg, 2003a).

- Florida State University reduced salaries by putting central faculty in charge of course development in its bachelor's degree programs and assigning mentors to interact with students (Boeke, 2004).

- Florida Virtual School increased its use of teaching adjuncts, which increased training and mentoring costs, but lowered salaries and overhead (Boeke, 2004).

- The University of Illinois allowed graduate assistants to teach courses and used undergraduate peer-tutors and peer-to-peer interactions to answer basic questions (Avran, Ory, Bullock, Burnaska, & Hanson, 2004).

- The University of Colorado–Boulder and the University of Buffalo are using undergraduate learning assistants in lieu of graduate assistants, because undergraduates are better at assisting their peers and can identify common learning errors for faculty to resolve (Twigg, 2003b).

- A Washington State University study found that spending additional time on planning courses decreases the time spent developing and delivering them (Boeke, 2004). (A more complete description of this study is provided later in this chapter.)

It is important to understand how economies of scale can affect an institution's ability to use online courses. An economy of scale requires that an institution spread the higher cost of course development among a greater number of students. In a traditional course, class size may be limited for various reasons (e.g., limits are placed on course enrollments by the terms of a union contract, or the chosen pedagogy works best with a smaller number of students). A traditional course can only become more efficient if the faculty member can take on more students. With online courses that are well designed (such as those that automate grading or instructional functions), faculty are better able to handle higher enrollment. Again, to justify the expense of designing online courses, the cost must be divided among a large group of students. In order to serve these groups, institutions must focus on designing high-enrollment courses and/or smaller enrollment courses that can be repeated often, without substantial upgrades.

Here are some ways institutions use online learning to achieve an economy of scale:

- Mega-universities enroll 2.8 million students at a cost of around $350 per student—versus $12,500 per U.S. student, on average, and $10,000 per UK student (Daniel, 1996).

- Four Georgia universities collaborated on online French courses after enrollment in face-to-face courses declined. The costs were higher than they had been for the traditional classes, but lower than offering several classes on several different campuses (Boeke, 2004).

- Community colleges participating in Washington Online realized additional savings by collaborating on student services and course development (Boeke, 2004).

- Old Dominion University (see www.dl.odu.edu) uses several technologies and a network of more than 50 partner institutions to offer its courses to more than 6,000 students throughout the U.S. and in the armed services.

The next section focuses on studies that have documented an improvement in quality or cost effectiveness.

Improving Costs and Student Learning

As previously noted, the 30 institutions that participated in the National Center for Academic Transformation Program in Course Redesign found that redesigning high-enrollment courses was extremely cost efficient. The institutions that participated in this project were also required to plan for and demonstrate improvements in student learning. Several of them found that online courses improved retention. Students who drop out of or withdraw from a traditional course may keep other students from enrolling and those who fail and retake traditional courses cost the institution money, since they require the repeated use of faculty time and institutional resources. By contrast, students who successfully learn the material so they can move on with their studies are a boon to the institution.

Among those institutions that participated in the course redesign project, a positive change was obvious. The University of Maine saw the drop-failure-withdrawal (DFW) rate for its introductory psychology class dip from 28% to 19%, while Drexel University's DFW rate for its computer programming class dropped from 49% to 38%. At Florida Gulf Coast University, the DFW for a fine arts class went from 45% to 11%, and the DFW for an introductory sociology class at Indiana

University–Purdue University Indianapolis dropped from 39% to 25%. These improvements make a strong case for redesigning courses with high DFW rates and courses that are critical gateways to important majors. A successful redesign enables an institution to serve more students, and existing students use resources more efficiently.

- With a 7% increase in course retention spawned by 25 redesigned sections, Central Florida University calculated that it could cut one section of its American government course, saving $28,064 every time that course was offered (Twigg, 2003b).

- At Brigham Young University, the content and learning outcomes of numerous sections taught by different instructors were made more consistent (Waddoups, Hatch, & Butterworth, 2003).

- Florida State University increased retention after it adopted a model that made central faculty responsible for course development and had mentors interact with students (Boeke, 2004).

- At the University of Central Florida, students in a redesigned political science course scored an average of 2.9 extra points, versus the 1.6-point gain achieved by students in the traditional course (Twigg, 2003b).

- At Pennsylvania State University, students in a redesigned course on statistics outperformed their peers in the traditional course (Twigg, 2003b).

- In a redesigned statistics course at Carnegie Mellon University, student performance on skill and concept tests increased 22.8% (Twigg, 2003b).

In 19 of the 30 course redesign projects, student learning improved (Twigg, 2003b). In the remaining projects, there was no significant difference.

How did these institutions achieve such improvements? For the most part, they followed the principles of improving efficiency by redesigning target courses so that they could be offered term after term (achieving an economy of scale), would require less faculty effort (substituting capital for labor), and could rely on tutors or assistants (substituting lower cost labor for higher cost labor). Different institutions used different designs and practices to achieve their ends, which proves that the principles can be used in highly individual ways.

The following essay illustrates the advantages of a cost analysis, as revealed by the findings of a recent Washington State University (WSU) study led by Gary Brown, the director of WSU's Center for Teaching, Learning, and Technology, and Tom Henderson, who was also employed by the Center for Teaching, Learning, and Technology when the study was conducted.

....

Insights Into Costs and Quality: A Study at Washington State University
Tom Henderson and Gary Brown

In 1999 the Center for Teaching, Learning, and Technology (CTLT) decided to field-test the Technology Costing Methodology (TCM). At approximately the same time, the Washington State Higher Education Coordinating (HEC) Board requested that WSU provide the board with an analysis of the costs of face-to-face courses, compared to those of online courses. Although the TCM study did not provide the clear and simple answers the HEC Board had hoped for, it did deepen our collective understanding of the costs (and outcomes) of technology-mediated instruction.

Washington State University Conducts the TCM Study

In fall 1999 the Washington State University Distance Degree Program (DDP) began offering online courses. Each of its 10 original classes was developed by a multidisciplinary team consisting of a faculty member or course developer and staff from the CTLT and DDP (Brown, Cook, & Henderson, 2001).

While pilot-testing the TCM procedures, WSU identified a subset of four key activities on which to focus its cost analysis: design, development, delivery, and assessment. (See table 2.2 [Henderson, Brown, & Meyers, 2003], which shows the average number of hours the team spent developing each course and the average number of students that enrolled each semester.) There are two key principles that we seek to incorporate in the design strategy of every course: 1) we strive to reuse existing educational resources whenever possible, and 2) we believe that facilitating student interaction is a central part of the course experience.

Table 2.2

Average Course Costs by Activity, Average Development Hours, and Students Enrolled

Design	$4,137
Develop	$4,019
Deliver	$4,891
Assess	$966
Total Cost	$14,013
Direct Hours	546
Students Enrolled	17

TCM proved to be very effective for estimating the costs of courses developed by a multidisciplinary team along several budget lines. Our task would have been much harder without using TCM or activity-based costing. One of the key findings of our initial study was that the cost of developing and delivering web-based courses was inversely proportionate to the amount of the investment in their design. We combined the TCM results with those of other studies being conducted at the same time to develop the following findings, which WSU has incorporated into subsequent course design processes.

Insight #1: Activity-Based Costing and Learning Outcomes

During the TCM field study, a parallel study was taking place at WSU—a formal assessment of faculty and student goals, activities, and processes (GAPs). GAPs began with a survey of instructors early in the term that asked them what their course goals were and how they planned to assess those goals. A survey was then administered to students, asking them their course goals, which methods of assessing their work they perceived as most effective, and questions designed to assess the learning processes taking place in the course. Several of the questions on learning processes were based on Chickering and Gamson's (1987) *Seven Principles for Good Practice in Undergraduate Education.*

Courses that participated in GAPs included distance courses that had been designed, distance courses that had not been designed, on-campus courses, and a few courses from other institutions that were using WSU's homegrown course management system. A regression analysis was then used to evaluate the survey responses from students in these different courses. As it turned out, students enrolled in courses that had been through a formal design process were significantly more likely to report learning experiences aligned with principles of good practice. Specifically, they reported that they:

- Received prompt feedback on course activities from instructors and/or peers

- Spent more time than expected on tasks

- Discussed course topics with others outside of class

- Learned in new ways that did not come easily

- Shared ideas and responded to the ideas of others

These were key insights, especially when viewed in the context of the TCM study. The school's investment in designing courses had saved them time and money while improving students' learning experiences. The authors of the studies began to realize that an ABC analysis not only provided them with cost estimates, but also with major insights into the process. The TCM analysis leverages costs in ways that can also evince quality gains.

Insight #2: Saving More Costs Through Design

The experience of conducting the TCM pilot study encouraged us to follow up with several subsequent costing studies, which found that courses that go through a design process (or even a quick review process) cost less to maintain and support. Designed courses also cost less to convert to new course management. This suggests that cost analysis and formal design or review processes are strategic investments that should not be considered one-off activities, but should instead be part of ongoing procedures.

Lessons Learned

One of the key lessons WSU learned from the TCM experience is that it is vital to include the amount spent on support and maintenance in any breakdown of course costs. The authors originally assumed that courses would not incur significant maintenance costs after the first time they were offered. They were wrong. The bulk of support and maintenance costs do occur during the initial offering, because the bugs are being worked out, faculty and students are learning new tools, and other improvements are being implemented. But courses that are not designed and developed, or reviewed for idiosyncrasies, are likely to cost more to maintain.

Another lesson learned is that activity-based costing data can be gathered more quickly (yet with just as much accuracy) by interviewing a few key managers. The authors of the TCM study interviewed 26 people, but in retrospect, the necessary information could have been gathered by interviewing just three or four midlevel managers. This is a key point, because one of the oft-cited disadvantages of activity-based costing is the amount of time it takes to conduct interviews. After all, when it comes to activity-based costing studies, "It is better to be approximately correct than precisely inaccurate" (Cokins, 2004).

Activity-based costing analysis is a versatile and useful tool that has been used for simple projects (e.g., restating departmental budgets) as well as more complex projects (e.g., estimating the costs and risks of alternative investments in course management systems).

Tom Henderson is currently director of testing and assessment at Central Washington University. Gary Brown is director of the Center for Teaching, Learning, and Technology at Washington State University.

Summing Up

WSU's commitment to continue analyzing its use of educational technologies in various courses is to be commended. By constantly examining course costs and student outcomes, its leaders have learned lessons that they can apply to course design in the future.

Too often, the issue of cost effectiveness is not considered until there is a specific request from an external source. This puts institutions at a disadvantage, as it allows other entities to set the agenda for their cost analysis. The resulting studies are often quickly, and sometimes poorly, designed. If there is an ongoing assessment of cost effectiveness and student outcomes already taking place at your institution, you will be better prepared to answer accountability requests. And—as WSU knows—you can also reap the benefits of applying what you have learned. Additional information on processes for achieving cost efficiencies can be found in Ward and Meyer (2006).

If your institution is facing a trio of challenges (rising demands, uncertain resources, and increased competition) and you want to use technology to find solutions, you would do well to try some of the approaches discussed in this chapter. Make a careful study of your institution's expenses, use the information to discover inefficiencies, and test different approaches to lowering costs. Also, find a way to design learning initiatives that are efficient and effective. This will help your institution meet challenges and allow more of your students to benefit from what you are doing.

Katrina A. Meyer is currently associate professor of higher and adult education at the University of Memphis. She is author of Cost-Efficiencies in Online Learning (Jossey-Bass, 2006), a part of the ASHE-ERIC Higher Education Report Series. For more than three years, she was director of distance learning and technology for the University and Community College System of Nevada and prior to this position, served 8 years as associate director of academic affairs, specializing in distance learning and telecommunications for the Higher Education Coordinating Board in the state of Washington. She has been a member of WCET since 1991, and was chair of the WCET Steering Committee in 1998–1999.

Russell Poulin is the associate director of WCET (www.wcet.info). Russ organizes the information sharing activities among WCET's members and directs EduTools.info, which provides independent reviews of educational software and courses. He consults on distance education planning projects, and serves on the editorial board of Innovate. For WCET Russ has codirected projects on interstate program sharing and on technology costing. Previously, Russ coordinated distance education activities for the North Dakota University System. Russ earned his bachelor's degree in mathematics and economics from the University of Colorado–Denver and a master's in statistics and research methodology from the University of Northern Colorado

References

Arvan, L., Ory, J. C., Bullock, C. D., Burnaska, K. K., & Hanson, M. (1998). The SCALE efficiency projects. *Journal of Asynchronous Learning Networks, 2*(2), 33–60.

Boeke, M. (Ed.). (2004). *Technology costing methodology casebook 2004.* Boulder, CO: Western Cooperative for Educational Telecommunications.

Brown, G., Cook, C., & Henderson, T. (2001). The costs of developing courses and teaching online. In M. Boeke (Ed.), *The technology costing methodology casebook 2001* (pp. 35–41). Boulder, CO: Western Cooperative for Educational Telecommunications.

Campbell, J. O., Bourne, J. R., Mosterman, P. J., Nahvi, M., Rassai, R., Brodersen, A. J., & Dawant, M. (2004). Cost-effective distributed learning with electronics labs. *Journal of Asynchronous Learning Networks, 8*(3), 5–10.

Chickering, A. W., & Gamson, Z. F. (1987, March). Seven principles for good practice in undergraduate education. *AAHE Bulletin, 39*(7), 3–7.

Cokins, G. (2004, March 20). If ABC is the answer then what is the question? In C. Geith & T. Henderson (Cohosts), *Planning and conducting your cost study* [Webcast]. TLT Group, WCET, & NACUBO.

Cukier, J. (1997). Cost-benefit analysis of telelearning: Developing a methodology framework. *Distance Education, 18*(1), 137–152.

Daniel, J. S. (1996). *Mega-universities and knowledge media: Technology strategies for higher education.* London, England: Kogan Page.

Fisher, S., & Nygren, T. I. (2000). *Experiments in the cost-effective uses of technology in teaching: Lessons from the Mellon program so far.* Retrieved July 13, 2006, from: http://www.ceutt.org/ICLT%20CEUTT.pdf

Henderson, T., Brown, G., & Myers, C. (2003). *Quality, efficiency, and course design.* Retrieved July 13, 2006, from: www.tltgroup.org/resources /F_Eval_Cases/WSU_ID.htm

Jones, D. (2004). *Technology costing methodology handbook—Version 2.0.* Boulder, CO: Western Cooperative for Educational Telecommunications

Levin, H. M., & McEwan, P. J. (2001). *Cost-effectiveness analysis: Methods and applications* (2nd ed.). Thousand Oaks, CA: Sage.

Massy, W. F. (2003). *Honoring the trust: Quality and cost containment in higher education.* Bolton, MA: Anker.

National Center for Higher Education Management Systems. (2002). *Projected state and local budget surplus (gap) as a percentage of revenues— 2013.* Retrieved July 13, 2006, from: http://higheredinfo.org/dbrowser /index.php?submeasure=197&year=2013&level=&mode=definitions &state=0

Russell, T. L. (1999). *No significant difference phenomenon: A comparative research annotated bibliography on technology for distance education.* Montgomery, AL: International Distance Education Certification Center.

Ruth, S. R. (2006). eLearning—A financial and strategic perspective. *EDUCAUSE Quarterly 29*(1), 22–30.

Twigg, C. A. (2003a). *Improving learning and reducing costs: Lessons learned from round I of the Pew Grant program in course redesign.* Troy, NY: Rensselaer Polytechnic Institute Center for Academic Transformation.

Twigg, C. A. (2003b, July/August). Improving quality and reducing cost: Designs for effective learning. *Change, 35*(4), 22–29.

Twigg, C. A. (2003c). Improving quality and reducing costs: New models for online learning. *EDUCAUSE Review, 38*(5), 28–38.

Waddoups, G. L., Hatch, G. L., & Butterworth, S. (2003). Balancing efficiency and effectiveness in first year reading and writing. In J. Bourne, & J. C. Moore (Eds.), *Elements of quality online education: Practice and direction: Vol. 4. Sloan-C series* (pp. 103–115). Needham, MA: Sloan-C.

Ward, K., & Meyer, K. A. (2006). *Cost efficiencies in online learning* (ASHE Higher Education Report, 32[1]). Washington, DC: George Washington University, Graduate School of Education and Human Development.

3 ··· Student Services, Rethought for All Students

Patricia (Pat) Shea

What do institutions do for students? They inform, assess, advise, instruct, evaluate, finance, house, and credential. With so many of these activities student services based, the time has come to give them the attention they deserve.

—Michael Tagawa, Leeward Community College

Educators have said for decades that student services are critical to student success and retention. For many campus-based students, however, access to services has been hit or miss, because long lines or limited hours make it difficult for them to be serviced. Off-campus students have been even more likely to be left out, unless distance or continuing education units provide outreach assistance.

Today, the web and other technologies are changing this for all students. As campuses increasingly put services online, many have begun to offer an experience similar to (or better) than that which they have offered face to face. They have also made the services more accessible.

As these changes occur, the important role played by student services is becoming much more visible. Just look at how many pages on your web site represent student services. As you peruse those pages, questions may begin to nag at you. What does "accessible" mean? What does "similar or better quality service" mean? And even more fundamentally, what does the term *student services* mean?

Let's start with the last question and work backwards.

What Are Student Services?

WCET struggled with the question of what constitutes student services early in its project, "Beyond the Administrative Core: Creating Web-Based Student Services for Online Learners," which was funded from

2000–2003 by the U.S. Department of Education. When WCET convened an initial meeting of its three partners in the project—Kansas
State University, Regis University (Colorado), and Kapi'olani
Community College (Hawaii)—there was no consensus on the meaning
of student services. Indeed, in one campus department there were four
different definitions of academic advising. In order to work together, we
had to come to a common understanding.

The result of that effort is captured in the web of student services dis-
played in Figure 3.1. The diagram kept us focused on that project and
has been very useful in a number of other projects. In the web of student services, services are divided into five categories: an administrative
core, an academic services suite, a communications suite, a student communities suite, and a personal services suite. Each suite contains several
services, though the dotted lines around the perimeter of the web indicate that they are not all inclusive.

Figure 3.1.
Web of Student Services

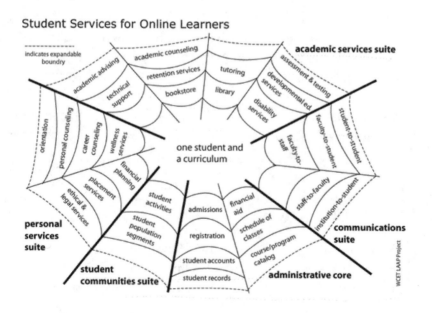

Student Services for Online Learners

Although individual campuses sometimes customize the web by adding and deleting services, ideally the center title—"one student and a curriculum"—remains constant. It draws our attention to the most important goal in designing and delivering services: They should be centered around (and customized to) the needs of each student.

Even though a student may not use all of these services, any one of them can play a critical role in the student's relationship with an institution and in his or her personal success. In other instances, it could be the overall experience of many of these services, integrated with each other and with the curriculum, that elicits a positive or negative reaction from the student.

What Does "Similar-Quality Service for All Students" Mean?

Many students who have been unable to come to campus have turned to distance learning or continuing education departments for support services. Separate admissions, registration, bookstore, and library services (among others) were developed and provided by the staffs of these units to better meet the needs of the nontraditional student.

In many cases, these services were of similar or better quality than the traditional services. They had to be designed to meet the needs of a more mature adult population who demanded services that were more convenient and efficient. Too often, however, other services—such as advising, tutoring, and tech support—fell into the laps of distance learning instructors. Some instructors did not have the time or interest to provide these services. For the off-campus student, it was (and still is, on some campuses) a game of chance.

You might wonder why so many campuses once took a separate approach to providing services, rather than just calling upon the mainstream student services staff. There are four primary reasons. First, student services staffs were often overloaded just trying to meet the needs of their face-to-face students. Second, many staffs did not understand (and had not received training on) how to best serve the typical distance learning student. Third, the student information and other data infrastructure systems that supported the mainstream campus operations were not flexible enough to accommodate distance enrollments with such services as rolling admissions and open-ended course registrations. And finally, some institutional cultures saw off-campus students as existing outside their core mission, so there was little centralized administrative support to serve a population that was often small and difficult to reach.

The good news is that many of these reasons for managing nontraditional student services separately have disappeared. As campuses begin to automate some of their routine student services tasks, they are also reducing staff workloads. Today's college population is more diverse, older, and—with the majority working part-time—campus-based students are more like the nontraditional student population of the past. Coincidentally, the student services staff has already adapted. The student records systems have grown up too, incorporating more flexibility to better accommodate a variety of students and programs. As many institutions experience explosive growth in online enrollment, this effort is now seen as mission critical.

As differences between traditional and nontraditional students continue to blur, many campuses are moving in the direction of putting services online for all students. Unfortunately, some campuses are taking the fast, easy, but not very effective route of simply "web-inizing" current face-to-face practices. Others, however, are taking time to assess the needs of all the students they serve, rethinking what services they want to deliver, and developing multiple, integrated ways to deliver them. By doing so, they are making the most of new technology and providing a higher quality, more holistic experience for all students.

What Does "Accessible" Mean?

As funding for financial aid has declined and tuitions have increased over the last few years, the percentage of part-time and working students has risen substantially. For many of these students, it is not practical to come to campus during nine-to-five business hours. For some of the off-campus learners who reside in other states or countries, it is impossible.

With declining budgets the norm for most institutions, and many campuses out of space, adding more offices to expand personnel is not an option. So how are campuses ensuring that their services are accessible? One of the easiest and most cost-effective ways is to put services on the web, which allows students to check their grades, run degree audits, register for courses, and buy books with the click of a mouse. By expanding these self-service options, campuses can come close to offering service 24/7 while freeing their personnel to perform more complex and personalized tasks.

Of course, some students will still need help from a live student service staff person outside of office hours. How do schools handle this? Some contract with staff to provide extended evening and weekend coverage from home via a Virtual Private Network (VPN) connection. This is how the University of North Carolina–Greensboro currently provides additional financial aid counseling. Other schools outsource these services to a third-party provider. This is how Broward County Community College offers tutoring and technical support to its students (see the essay by Russ Adkins at the end of this chapter).

Should all services be accessible 24/7? No. It's not realistic. Although banks make many self-service options permanently available on the web, they also restrict certain services to phone or face-to-face interactions during business hours. Institutions must increasingly compete for students, and the availability of services does make a difference. It is best to make as many services available 24/7 as you can, whether through the Internet, email, or phone. It is also important to set appropriate student expectations for other services. A good example to follow is that of Athabasca University, which publishes its "Expect the Best" standards on its web site (see www.athabascau.ca/misc/expect). By clearly stating what services require human interaction or processing during business days, and telling students how long it will be before they can expect a response, Athabasca University better serves its whole community.

If you establish such standards, you must ensure that they are enforced. As part of our research, we tested response time for various services across several institutions. It was not uncommon to get an email response from one department in 24 hours, but wait several days or weeks to hear from another. In some cases, there was no response at all—even after a few months. At one institution, for example, we found that a student had to wait up to six months for the evaluation of his transfer credits. That student may have completed all of his courses for graduation but still had to wait until the end of the next term to graduate, which forced him to repeatedly call the registrar to check on his status. This is not good student service! By contrast, another institution promised and delivered transcript evaluations—including those for international courses—within 24 hours. Which school would you want to attend?

What Do Students Really Want?

Students expect an institution to offer online service that is similar or better than what they get from social, medical, and commercial outlets. They expect the following from their institution.

Self-Service

Younger students in particular want to serve themselves. Institutions that develop more self-service options reduce their staff's overall workload, freeing them to focus on the more important individualized services students prefer. This also enables institutions to provide expanded access to certain services, in some cases making them available 24/7. At Brigham Young University (BYU), students use a web-based "financial path to graduation" service to create a customized budget and find out how long it would take to pay back certain loans, given the typical salaries for jobs associated with their majors, inflation, and other factors. As a result, BYU students have significantly reduced their borrowing in recent years. In addition, by automating some of the services associated with financial aid, BYU has freed its financial aid staff from routine tasks, making it possible for all of them to become certified financial planners. The staff can now offer a much higher level of service to its students.

Just-in-Time

Students have grown accustomed to securing instructions, information, and advice as they need it, rather than all at once, as in the past. The Internet enables institutions to meet their expectations with concise packets of service at specific or on-demand intervals preferred by the student. Regis University staff, for example, worked with DataTel, the manufacturer of the school's student information system, to automate some of the tasks and communications associated with applicants to its School for Professional Studies. Prospective students can now login to see where they stand in the admissions process. Automated email messages alert them to missing recommendations or other documents and provide them with just-in-time instructions to help them prepare for their first academic advising appointment. Hundreds of hours of unnecessary telephone conversations have been eliminated, and students come to their appointments better prepared to discuss more important topics such as choosing a major.

Personalized Service

In the era of computers, generic service is obsolete. Students want and expect to be recognized as individuals. Portal technology makes this possible on even the largest campuses. For example, Collage, a Kent State University career portfolio (see https://collage.kent.edu/guest), is a web-based, interactive learning tool that engages students in self-directed exercises to foster self-awareness, enhance career exploration, and facilitate decision-making. Students set goals, identify their strengths and abilities, and complete exercises that help them focus on a major or career. They can then revisit and update their Collages as they progress toward graduation. By developing a personalized Collage, students are able to document their experiences in a reflective and meaningful way, enhancing their ability to select and effectively prepare for a rewarding career.

Customized Service

Since today's postsecondary population is more diverse than ever before, one size does not fit all. Students increasingly expect institutions to deliver services tailored to their specific needs or interests. Institutions that manage this relationship well will set themselves apart from the competition. In its WCET project, Kapi'olani Community College focused its development efforts on one group of students—those enrolled in an online medical assisting program. Staffers filled a portal with information and services specifically customized to the needs of this particular group. Students could then login and take a series of assessments to help them determine which career they might be most interested in (or best suited for), whether it was that of an X-ray technician, a dental hygienist, or something else. Students could also find links to scholarship and loan information that specifically targeted those in their field. They could link to an established list of library resources supporting their coursework. They could participate in tutoring modules designed to help them apply the principles they learned in math class to knowledge needed for their practicum, such as calculating drug dosages, or pronouncing and spelling medical terms. They could pop into a live chat with an academic advisor or seek assistance from a career counselor. All of these services were customized to these students' needs and available in one place. (To find out more about this effort, see the essay by Michael Tagawa.)

Customizable Services

"Choice" is the watchword of this era, and using it effectively is necessary to prevent information overload. Students want to choose their formats, views, and preferred services for easy access at their fingertips. In one recent example, Kansas State University used its institutionally developed course management system to create a web interface between

DARS, its academic advising degree audit system, and several other systems that store student information. Students can now login and run their own degree audit while choosing different formats to display that information, collapsing and expanding views as they wish. Their ability to customize this service provides more control to students in rural areas with slow connections or those who wish to print only certain sections of a report. These students can also run "what-if" scenarios to see what courses they would need if they were to change their major.

Push-and-Pull Choices or Selections

New technologies make it possible to collect and send information or services to students as needed. Students increasingly expect institutions to "push" reminders, relevant information, and other services to them as appropriate. For example, a student using iCan, the integrated counseling and advising network at North Carolina's Central Piedmont Community College, is able to login and participate in a live chat whenever a counselor is available (see www1.cpcc.edu/ican). The counselor can then use push technologies to send specific web pages to the student. If the counselor is not available, the student can leave an email message and expect a response within 24 hours when school is in session. Services through iCan are often available until midnight.

Interactive Information Exchanges

Students (especially those who play web games) increasingly expect interactive pages that take them quickly to the specific information or services they desire. Whether this is done through "smart paths" on the site or pop-up windows that feature live chats and instant messaging, students prefer sites that allow them to communicate or get information in a real-time environment. At the University of Arizona, an interactive web map lets students choose the information they want to display, selecting from specific buildings, handicap-accessible entrances and restrooms, nearby parking, emergency phones, local bus routes, and areas under construction (see http://iiewww.ccit.arizona.edu/uamap/map.asp) Users can zoom in or out, search for various buildings, or use MapQuest to get driving directions.

Integrated and Consistent Services

Good student service calls for blending related services to provide a seamless and unified experience for students. All too often, multiple departments post the same information, but one department does it better than the other! (Or worse: The information in one department conflicts with that in the other.) It is fairly common to find information about what a student can do with a particular major—as posted by the academic advising department—also posted on the career counseling department's pages.

By working together, multiple units can develop and link to one robust source of information, saving their employees' time and better serving their students. Institutions can deliver more integrated and consistent services if they team up across the "silos" to work on style and writing guides for the web site, use content management software and strategies, and assign responsibility for the maintenance of web pages in job descriptions. At Arizona State University, students can login to create a four-year plan that includes course sequences. They can then seamlessly run that plan against the degree audit system or activate it to register for appropriate classes next term. Since their work on the plan is constantly being updated and stored, their progress toward graduation is always clear.

New Models

As campuses have grown, we've seen numerous student services added in an ad hoc fashion as the need arose. As a result, many student services operate in their own silos, with separate technology infrastructures and different policies and procedures, confined by separate physical spaces and incompatible data systems. Today's technology makes it possible to adopt different models that are more effective for the student and the institution.

Let's look at two interesting models: the one-stop service center and program-level services.

....

One-Stop Service Center
Darlene Burnett

The kind of information and services students receive helps shape how successful and satisfying their college or university experience will be. Those who work in student services know the tremendous impact information and services can have on students, as well as how the institution is regarded by parents, legislators, and other key stakeholders. Today's students are busy and expect a higher level of customer service than ever before. The degree to which institutions meet—or exceed—those expectations has an impact on recruitment, retention, and alumni loyalty.

Institutions that have focused on the one-stop service center approach understand the principles of customer service and realize the importance of redesigning the processes for the improved delivery of services. Their vision of student services is student centered in its processes and interactions. We used to think of service interactions only in terms of the transaction involved, but we have since learned that we don't just deliver service—we deliver intangible experiences that engage and involve the student on an emotional level. Every "touch point" a student has with an institution adds to or subtracts from his or her experience. Taken as a whole, these touch points help shape the student's enduring relationship with the institution.

For example, consider a student who contacts the institution with the same question or issue via phone, email, and in person. Will the student be able to go to a one-stop physical or virtual center to get an answer or will the student get the runaround? Will the student's experience be consistent? Will it be positive? Will this interaction add to the positive side of the student's relationship with the institution? What emotion will be evoked by this transaction?

Many institutions are being asked to provide improved services for an expanding number of students, but have no additional budget. Many even have a reduced budget. When that happens, it is critical that more services be delivered over the Internet, freeing up staff to help students with difficult problems. We need to eliminate the current requirements for information intermediation by staff. For example, Kapi'olani Community College found that when it assessed the roles of staff and divided all interaction into three categories (transact/operate, plan/analyze, and advise/counsel), the result was a model that corresponded to 70%, 20%, and 10%. By shifting 70% of student services to the Internet for self-service, staffers trained as generalists in a one-stop center can focus on the more complex 20%, while staff specialists can deal with the remaining 10%—the most difficult issues.

As campuses focus on this one-stop approach, they must integrate their various methods of service delivery and redesign their information and processes from the students' perspective. The term *one-stop service* encompasses physical one-stop centers, virtual one-stop web portals, and one-stop phone or help desks. Central to each of these delivery methods is a rethinking of how information is presented in an interaction with the student/customer. One of the primary benefits of creating one-stop services is the elimination of the runaround that students experience. This change leads to improved customer service and satisfaction.

There are several physical one-stop service models. The University of Delaware and Boston College have a central one-stop center, while the University of Minnesota–Twin Cities has central and satellite one-stop centers. Although different institutions have taken different approaches to creating physical one-stop centers, one-stop web portals, and one-stop call centers, there is a central theme that is required to make any version of one-stop centers successful. The common thread among best-practice institutions is that they have redesigned and integrated multiple service functions. For example, registration, financial aid, and student accounts may all be integrated into a one-stop enrollment center.

The institutions that most successfully redesign and integrate their services usually start by examining what is driving the need for change. Before jumping in and making changes, they ask themselves: "What do students want and expect?" Their understanding results in new processes, redesigns, alternative facilities, and web-based applications.

Critical success factors for any project of significant change in the area of student services include:

- Use of a cross-functional team (students included)

- Executive sponsorship

- Communication, communication, communication

- Implementation of change management

- Marketing of the initiative to internal stakeholders and external stakeholders

The creation of innovative student-centered services is not a one-time project. It requires an ongoing commitment to one-stop services from institution executives. There is no single one-stop service model that's right for every institution. Each institution must work with a cross-functional team (that includes students) to ask the necessary questions about existing services and expectations and create the one-stop services that best fit its unique culture and values. If an institution already has one-stop services on the Internet, then in-person, one-stop centers should be developed next (or vice versa).

Students want convenient, accurate, and friendly access to services. One-stop models have successfully met those needs.

Darlene Burnett is principal in Burnett & Associates, consulting for institutions on the design of student-centered services.

As mentioned earlier, students want services that are customized to their needs. Kapi'olani Community College (KCC) was an early leader in thinking about how web services could be designed to support a particular community of students. The college's project leader, Michael Tagawa—then KCC's dean of health/legal education, library, and technology—described his institution's initial objective in the WCET project as developing templates for online tutoring. More complex objectives evolved over time. When the project partners determined that they would focus on a more student-centered, scalable, accessible, and "smart" model for delivering services, it became apparent that a template web-based model for tutoring represented a simplistic first-generation approach.

Kapi'olani Community College's final objective was to develop services that would increase the likelihood of a student achieving his or her academic objective. This was a major transition in thought, reflecting what the college needed to accomplish in terms of a student outcome rather than the simple establishment of a particular service. The major challenge was that a more comprehensive system of learning support required not only the development of a technological solution to the delivery of a service, but the transformation of the organization itself in terms of providing support.

The following essay describes KCC's vision for these services and the prototype it built.

E-Services at the Program Level
Michael Tagawa

Kapi'olani Community College (KCC) in Honolulu, Hawaii, is a community college that serves more than 7,000 students each year.

At the time the WCET Student Services project began in 2000, approximately 1.5% of the total student body participated in distance learning opportunities. Almost 70% of the students enrolled in distance learning courses were also enrolled in campus-based courses. The remaining 30% of students were located on neighboring islands, on other campuses in Oahu, or out of state. Distance enrollments were primarily concentrated in health programs such as medical assisting and emergency medical services.

The Problem

KCC provides education and training for a wide range of healthcare workers within the state. Programs and courses are delivered to students in high schools, those about to enter a college program, those in health career programs, and those in the incumbent workforce. Delivery methods include distance and traditional coursework at each of these four educational levels. A variety of structural problems prevented an optimum flow of students through this workforce pipeline, adversely affecting the college's responsiveness to community needs. These problems affected the program's efficiency and student quality. The most significant problems were in the following areas.

Course-based learning structures. The fundamental unit of student learning was the course, which assessed student competencies in aggregate. As a result, it was difficult to guarantee student competence in each area upon course completion. In addition, course competencies tended to focus on professional requirements and were often inadequate in addressing learning skills, the affective domain, and collateral workplace/student skills. In effect, the traditional assessment of student learning occurred at the tree level, overlooking the leaves and branches that made up the tree.

Program structures. At the start of the project, the articulation of the student learning experience between the four educational levels was weak at best. Even at the program level, with a broader range of learning support services, there was a need to better integrate the student learning experience between courses. In this case, because the student learning experience concentrated on individual trees, a vision of the forest was sometimes lacking.

Learning Relationships. Educational institutions often perceive themselves as providers of knowledge rather than facilitators of learning, which tends to establish teacher/learner (knowledge-bearer /knowledge-receiver) relationships. Although curricular and instructional structures are efficient and useful ways to guide the learning relationship, they sometimes overlook the fact that learning can and does occur outside the classroom, often without the presence of a teacher. Returning to the forest metaphor, trees do have an ability to grow without ever-present gardeners. To more effectively meet the state's workforce requirements for healthcare, KCC needed to focus its learning support services effort on addressing structural flaws within its programs.

The Vision

Resource constraints at the college prevented traditional learning support methods from being scaled upwards. The development of online learning support services provided an alternative method of service delivery. It was suggested, however, that to be effective, these support services needed to be developed strategically and targeted at the structural flaws of traditional education.

The vision being proposed was not a technological solution, but rather an organizational strategy for delivering learning assistance at the program level.

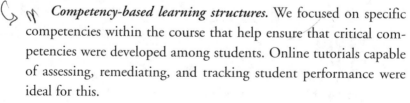 *Competency-based learning structures.* We focused on specific competencies within the course that help ensure that critical competencies were developed among students. Online tutorials capable of assessing, remediating, and tracking student performance were ideal for this.

The college initially developed tutorials designed to:

- Perform work skills assessments, skills development, and tracking

- Focus on applied competencies not adequately addressed by prerequisite courses (health-related math skills, for example, or anatomy topics not adequately covered by introductory math/anatomy and physiology courses)

Program-based communities. An online community was perceived to be essential to the delivery of online learning support services. The concept of a program-based online community implied a mechanism through which communication could occur among students, faculty, advisors, and the public, all of whom were in some manner tied to a particular academic program.

The online community provided a thread that connected and created learning experiences at the program level, above the course level. Initially, the college would use the program-based community to:

- Inform (through a program-specific calendar or bulletin)

- Manage program-level learning experiences (through the program-level coordination of service-learning)

- Provide learning assistance (through peer tutoring/mentoring)

- Permit random/personal communications between students to foster student community building (through bulletin boards/emails)

Multiple learning relationships. Due to resource constraints, the scalability of online learning support services could be achieved only through automation (tutorials) or student involvement and management of community activities.

Goals

To accomplish the project vision, a number of goals were established as the project evolved.

Goal 1. Develop a program-based model of learning support to supplant the traditional course-based model associated with tutoring. The reasoning behind this is that students' achievement of educational objectives was determined to be more than the sum of its parts (e.g., individual courses). It was a complex mix of learning activities and student-institution interactions that transcended individual courses.

Goal 2. Integrate academic and nonacademic learning support. The rationale behind this goal was that student achievement of educational objectives included learning at the course level (academic), but also incorporated nonacademic learning activities. At a community college, nonacademic learning activities are probably as critical to student success as academic activities. Key nonacademic learning activities included advising and foundational learning skills.

Goal 3. Deliver services 24/7, on demand, to all students.

Goal 4. Employ communication tools via a portal that creates a program-based learning support community. Normally, the learning support system is designed for individual students and structured around their majors. A variety of learning support models employing different communication/learning tools was developed to come as close as possible to emulating the rich learning environment that a student experiences, but in a manner that enables scalability and accessibility through the use of technology.

Accomplishments

A working portal-based prototype was developed for the medical assisting program using MetaDot portal freeware. The prototype was designed to demonstrate the various elements that can be brought together for learning support within a program, and to serve as a model for KCC and the University of Hawaii once the system-wide portal was implemented. The general framework of the prototype provided some standardization of learning support, but also allowed each program the flexibility to customize content materials.

The key elements of the learning support portal included the following:

- *Advising support.* Tutorials guided students through a structured exploration of career, job, academic program, and financial aid scenarios. Some of these "tutorials" were links to noninstitutional web sites (for career/financial aid exploration), or to materials developed by the college (for program exploration) and in partnership with various industries (for job exploration).

- *Academic learning support.* A variety of portal-based tools was assembled to provide interactive communication between the students and their program, including a discussion board, calendar, and news feed, as well as online tutorials, email, and online references. Learning support could then occur in a variety of ways: between instructor/counselor and student, student and student, or student and instructor.

- *Foundation skills support.* Online assessments and remediation for learning skills not explicitly covered by program curricula were addressed in part through this mechanism.

The following major organizational changes have occurred:

- *Improved integration of academic and nonacademic learning support.* Developing a portal required the coordination of academic learning support services and student services centered around the college experience. This was a departure from the college's traditional, nonintegrated approach to delivering these services. The initial demonstration project marked a strong start, but much more remains to be done to prepare the program to fully utilize the capabilities on which the project is modeled (for example, the way that an instructor provides learning support, the way a counselor advises, and what learning support they deliver).

- *A strengthened culture of assessment.* Although health programs have historically had a strong culture of assessment due to external certification and special accreditation, this has been strengthened to include the assessment of nonacademic skills. This has been an area of traditional weakness in the health programs, as reported by employers. KCC was the first in the community college system to pilot formal, national foundation skill standards-based assessments and is in the process of formalizing this in curricula. The models developed are beginning to spread to other program areas within the college and throughout the system.

Challenges

The project experienced a variety of challenges—some organizational, others technical in nature. The following major challenges were faced:

- *Funding.* The original funding model was probably adequate for the initial objective of developing simple web-based tutoring templates. However, funding became inadequate as the model evolved into a more enterprise-level model of learning support that employed program-based templates for student-institution interaction and integration of services. Additional sources of funding were necessary to acquire more enterprise-level technical solutions for the production and delivery of these services beyond the scope of the grant.

- *Technology.* KCC was undergoing a transition to a new student information system (SIS) and portal, a process that was in constant flux over the three years of the grant. This presented many challenges in terms of reallocating staff to support these changes and dealing with uncertainty in product development. Nevertheless, the project's identification of the functionality desired with online learning support services enabled the college to develop a prototype learning support system independent of a specific technology. The remaining challenge lay in integrating the elements of the prototype into the new SIS/portal over the course of a year or two. This would probably require some definition of a nonacademic learning assessment in the official student record.

- *Organizational.* Because of the uncertainty about the technology and the magnitude of organizational change involved, the project focused on one program area for testing. This enabled product development to progress faster. The downside of this approach, however, was the uncertainty over whether the elements associated with the prototype would transfer to other programs at the college. The college embarked on an institution-wide discussion on student advising, and elements from this project were presented as the primary tools for delivering those services.

Lessons Learned

- *Focus on function.* The project's emphasis on the functionality of services enabled the project team to navigate through technological uncertainty and slow organizational adaptation to change. In many respects, this emphasis led the team to focus on functional learning support tools that were adaptable to technology and independent of organizational structure.

- *Cultural change is slow.* Developing this project took a combination of pushing and pulling. The thinking evolved around the use of technology to deliver support services online. At times, the institution pushed the technology; at other times, the technology pulled it along. There was still resistance, but there was also the growing realization that web-based services are here to stay. The more progressive elements of the college moved to adopt and adapt the model in a variety of ways.

- *Technology requirements.* The development of online learning support services requires a robust technology infrastructure. In addition to the acquisition of a more robust student information system/portal, the campus technology infrastructure had to be upgraded significantly.

Summary

Kapiʻolani Community College developed a learning support system for students in the medical assisting program. Because it used portal technology, it offered a personalized and customized interface and a variety of features, including a calendar, orientation materials, a section for program communities, and sections for tutoring and advising. (It included orientation and advising because they were reclassified to be instances of nonacademic tutoring.) It also offered an interactive advising tutorial that guided premedical assisting students through the program's admissions process; ACT's WorkKeys® testing and KeyTrain™ tutoring for soft skills; and tutoring modules on the rules and pronunciation of key medical terms, dosage calculations, and introduction to the use of KCC's course management system. In addition, an anatomy tutorial was developed, and a peer mentoring system was devised so that second-year medical assisting students could be the first responders to questions that first-year medical assisting students posted on the bulletin board.

The KCC staff used MetaDot portal freeware to develop this prototype for a learning support service. This approach to learning support and its technical infrastructure became models for the rest of KCC and the University of Hawaii system as they implemented a new student information system and portal.

Michael Tagawa is the interim assistant dean of career and tech educa-
tion at Leeward Community College in Hawaii. Prior to that, he was
the dean of health/legal education, library, and technology services at
Kapi'olani Community Colleges.

Unique Services for Off-Campus Students

In addition to the services that both on- and off-campus students require, distance students have a unique need for such services as orientation to distance learning. They also need services or communication strategies that provide a sense of community. Without the orientation, students often underestimate the amount of time required for a distance course or program and the self-motivation required to be successful.

While most institutions have developed a variety of ways to involve students in campus activities, many distance learners can't come to campus. How, then, do you keep them engaged and make them feel that they are a part of the campus community? Let's look at how these services are provided online at Montgomery College in Maryland.

Online Student Success Center and Online Companion
Anita Crawley

Montgomery College (MC) is a three-campus, comprehensive community college located outside of Washington, DC. Distance learning enrollments have grown 20% each year from 2000–2005, but online student success—as measured by the As, Bs, or Cs earned in a course—has lagged behind on-campus success by 10%–12%. Since the array of online courses does not duplicate the array of face-to-face courses, it is possible the results may be skewed. Nevertheless, as with all students at the college, MC is looking for ways to improve the success of online students.

Online Student Success Center

At MC we have found that online students need information at three separate stages in the enrollment process. In stage one potential online learners must decide whether online learning is right for them. One of the resources they can access to help them is the Online Student Success Center, a web site available to all from the college's home page (see www.montgomerycollege.edu/Departments /distlrng). Students can find information there about the advantages and disadvantages of online learning and an overview of distance learning at MC.

In stage two a student enrolls in an online course. Here the Online Student Success Center offers additional resources to prepare students for their first class. MC online students must be familiar with MyMC, their student portal, and WebCT, the course management system. The Online Student Success Center provides a quick explanation and a more in-depth tutorial about how to access and navigate MyMC and WebCT.

For students in stage three, the center provides modules with content information and links to resources outside MC where students can learn about technical skills, effective online communication, and learning styles, as well as online writing, math, and study skills. To overcome personal barriers to online success, students have access to tips on time and stress management, organizational skills, and managing the potential isolation of learning online. Academic support includes topics such as library and Internet research, GPA calculators, online study skills, and procrastination. Because online students need some of the same resources as on-campus students, they will find links to those resources from this page, as well as to academic, career, and transfer advising for new and currently enrolled students.

The Online Student Success Center is a gateway to a wealth of information designed to help online students learn what to expect from online courses and complete them successfully. MC does not offer a formal orientation for online students, but its success center is viewed as one form of orientation to online learning.

Online Companion

The Online Companion: A Student's Guide to Success is a free, ongoing workshop that is facilitated throughout the year by the distance learning counselor at MC. The Online Companion site, which uses WebCT, includes information similar to that of the Online Student Success Center, but presented so that it replicates an online course. The Online Companion uses all of the WebCT communications tools, including its discussion board, WebCT email, and chat functions.

One week before the first day of the semester, all students and faculty with a WebCT account are given access to the Online Companion. The Online Companion, which was implemented in fall 2004, currently has more than 6,000 people enrolled. Students who go to their MyWebCT entry page find the Online Companion as a link in the Support Section, which also includes the WebCT Student User's Manual. The Online Companion is available to those who participate in online courses, blended courses, and on-campus courses supplemented by WebCT.

The Online Companion includes 12 content modules with information that helps acclimate students to online learning. Some modules encourage students to explore WebCT, experiment with the discussion board, take mock quizzes, and practice uploading course assignments. Other modules present academic advising and counseling content that helps them set goals and get educational, career, and transfer information. Students can read the modules, take self-assessments, and interact with the distance learning counselor who facilitates the web site.

A major objective of the Online Companion is to create a community where online students can connect with each other. Semesters begin with students introducing themselves to one another.

Students new to online learning are typically apprehensive, a concern that is addressed either by some of the seasoned online students or the workshop facilitator. A discussion thread is set up for each content module. The thread begins with a question intended to facilitate conversation about the topic. A Student Lounge is provided for open discussion, with threads for Ask a Counselor, Ask a Teacher, and Ask a Student Support Specialist.

There are currently more than 500 discussion messages on the discussion board. As a distance learning counselor, it is great to be able to publicly answer general advising and online learning questions. The hope is that others will read the information and realize that they can seek answers about their own situation. When a question requires access to a student's record, the discussion is taken offline to WebCT email.

As with traffic in the on-campus counseling and advising offices, students tend to appear at our door (or portal) just before and after the beginning of the semester and when it comes time to plan for the next semester. The following WebCT statistics show how often students use the Online Companion in an 18-month term. During the most recent term, 71% visited 10–49 times, 15% visited 50–99 times, 10% visited 100–199 times, and 4% visited more than 200 times. We definitely have a few regulars.

Throughout the year, information is updated on the announcement page and the campus news thread. Students are encouraged to post their favorite academic and nonacademic web sites.

The distance learning office promotes the web site, while the distance learning counselor encourages faculty to include contact information for the Online Companion and the distance learning counselor in their syllabi. The distance learning counselor is someone who has been selected to work with online students and who intervenes when they are not succeeding in their courses. As traffic for this service increases, other counselors will be needed to help support it.

A demo site for the Online Companion is available at http://webct.montgomerycollege.edu/. The username and password are guest_nb.

Instructor-Developed Orientations

Online instructors at Montgomery College are responsible for developing orientations for their students. Some have created on-campus orientations, while others have developed online orientations that they deliver from inside WebCT during the first week of the semester. The distance learning office, in collaboration with the counselors, faculty, and consultants who assist in supporting online learning at MC, is planning to develop "orientation to online learning" files that can be uploaded to each faculty WebCT site. We are also considering the development of a generic on-campus orientation for first-time online learners who would like a face-to-face opportunity to learn about the demands of online learning and find out how to navigate WebCT.

It is essential to offer a variety of ways to orient students to this relatively new way of learning. Some students are still laboring under the misconception that online courses are easier than on-campus courses. We hope that through on-campus information sessions about online learning, students will gain a more accurate understanding of the demands of learning at a distance and will make more educated decisions about whether or not online learning is right for them.

Montgomery College will continue to develop ways to integrate our students into the fabric of the school. We believe that more engagement will lead to improved rates of online course success.

Anita Crawley is the distance learning counselor at Montgomery College and the developer of the Online Student Success Center and Online Companion.

Implementing Web Services

Putting services online has become easier as new technologies and programs become more user friendly and there is less resistance to web-based services and transactions. Some campuses have done a better job than others. Even within one institution, some services are better than others!

What makes the difference? Early results from the Center for Transforming Student Services' audit tool—discussed later in this chapter—indicate that there are several factors at play. First among them is leadership—having someone at the top say that putting good student services online is important, and then providing the necessary support to make it happen. Second, institutions need a vision for their services that has been crafted from the student's point of view. This should be part of an institution's strategic plan, carefully developed with wide input from staff, faculty, and students. (Don't forget the students—it is amazing how many do!)

It is also important to have a creative staff who are willing to do things differently. As we researched the best practices in online student services, we were intrigued by how many online student services could be found at campuses with limited resources. One good example is the program-level service designed for medical assisting students at Kapi'olani Community College as described earlier. Of course, having adequate funding makes any job easier—but too often, a lack of funds is simply used as a convenient excuse.

During the WCET student services project, staff authored a set of guidelines[1] to help campuses put student services online (Shea & Armitage, 2003). The guidelines include more than 40 lessons we learned in designing and implementing web services, including the most common mistake: rushing to find a solution before you really know what you want your new service to be like.

Assuming that your campus has involved all of its stakeholders and students in deciding what new web services should include, there are several options to consider when you develop them. These include buying a solution, building it in house, collaborating with others, or outsourcing.

Campuses have lots of experience with the first two options when it comes to student services, but less so with the last two. This is partly due to the historical nature of higher education as a cottage industry, in which each institution (until recently) has had to do its own thing. These days, new technologies make it easier to collaborate with other institutions when developing and providing web-based student services. It has also become simpler to outsource to a third-party provider—so seamless, in fact, that the student may never know that the service is not coming directly from his or her campus.

Embracing these options will require some institutions to make a difficult culture shift. Others may see this as the wave of the future, especially in an era of trying to do more with less. A number of states (including Connecticut, Minnesota, and Kentucky) and systems (including the University of Texas, UT Telecampus) have taken the lead by working with local institutions to create collaborative one-stop distance learning initiatives that provide centralized services to students. Many institutions have joined hands in outsourcing certain services, using their collective bargaining power to secure more attractive contracts than they could on their own. An interesting collaborative model that goes beyond some of these boundaries is FACTS, Florida's online academic advising system, which was developed by the state's Department of Education. Not only does the system serve Florida's college students, it also supports high school students who are making the transition to college.

Building a Statewide Student Advising System
Andrea Latham and Connie Graunke

FACTS.org is Florida's one-stop online statewide student advising system. FACTS is an acronym for Florida Academic Counseling and Tracking for Students. The system was designed by the Florida

Department of Education to provide maximum access and seamless articulation services to help high school and college students make informed choices about their education. Launched in 2000, FACTS.org offers a comprehensive suite of services that gives users the unique ability to get all the information they need in one place. On our web site, users can monitor their high school progress, learn about postsecondary opportunities in Florida, explore careers, apply for college admission and financial aid, choose a major, and track their progress toward a college degree.

The original concept for FACTS.org was born from a legislative mandate passed by the Florida legislature in 1995. The legislation called for the state university system and community college system to produce a "single, statewide computer-assisted student advising system, which must be an integral part of the process of advising, registering, and certifying students for graduation" (Florida Statutes, §1007.28 [2004]). In order to accomplish this mandate, an online infrastructure had to be created that would allow college students to access their transcripts, shop for degrees at public institutions, assess their progress toward a degree, and assess the impact of changing majors or institutions.

At the time a board of regents governed the 10 universities, while the 28 community colleges were separately managed and funded entities governed by the state board of community colleges. Each state institution had implemented a wealth of different systems. The universities had a shared advising system infrastructure called SASS (derived from the DARS system used at Ohio's Miami University), while the community colleges were just starting to develop an infrastructure when the legislation was passed. Each institution had developed its own admissions, registration, financial aid, and fee payment systems. The community colleges were divided into five different consortia, with each consortium sharing development and maintenance costs for its own set of systems. Given this type of statewide organization, the prospect of bringing together the institutions in an organized manner seemed unmanageable!

The legislature was concerned about three trends: 1) the trend for college students to take five or six years to complete an undergraduate degree, 2) the trend for students to take more hours than needed for graduation (the two were clearly related), and 3) the development of distance learning. Several initiatives were passed to address the issue of excess hours, but it soon became clear that these initiatives would not be enough to speed students through the system. In addition, as distance learning became more prevalent, it also became clear that students would need a web-based method of finding eligible degree programs and courses and a way to receive accurate advising information online.

In the summer of 1996, the board of regents and the state board of community colleges hosted several focus groups with administrators, faculty, students, and parents to gather information about user expectations and requirements for a statewide system. The real purpose of forming these groups lay in trying to decide which would be better: a centralized system—where all the institutions fed into a central source—or a distributed system. A number of existing systems at different institutions were considered for their potential to serve as templates for the new system, along with many commercial, off-the-shelf solutions. Each had interesting and innovative characteristics, but none offered a complete solution. What's more, individual institutions expressed considerable opposition to converting to a centralized system. In the end, concerns over data responsibility, currency of information, and control of business rules all influenced the decision to move toward a distributed model.

A pilot project was devised to provide a proof of concept before proceeding with concrete plans (including funding) for the development of a statewide system. The secretary of the Department of Management Services (DMS) was the pilot project manager. It was a logical choice, as DMS was responsible for the state's communications infrastructure, and the secretary was a member of a new state entity formed to foster and coordinate distance learning activities in the state. The pilot was funded by dollars allocated to Florida's distance learning initiative.

It was deemed important to have a working pilot by the start of the 1997 legislative session, so funding could be considered for that year's budget. Since we had only three months to make the deadline, DMS hired several consulting agencies to assist six designated pilot institutions with implementation. In spite of having to deal with the disorganization of many participants, as well as policy issues, hardware issues, and a general lack of consensus, a working pilot was completed at the end of three months—one that demonstrated the technical feasibility of a statewide system.

The original pilot was a learning experience and a necessary part of getting the statewide system to where it is today. We took what we learned from that pilot and began to build on those experiences to create a solid design for the "real" system. In 1998 the Florida Legislature approved the project plan and appropriated funding. Each postsecondary division appointed board members to govern the project, as well as academic and technical experts to advise the board. With the board in place, the Florida Center for Advising and Academic Support (FCAAS) was established at the University of South Florida to carry out the development and implementation of the system.

In the beginning the committee submitted a request for proposal to find a vendor or vendors that could supply us with a software solution to tie the institutional academic advising systems together under a distributed model. None of the vendors had a total workable solution, so we decided to use our own resources to program a solution with four prototype institutions. Each prototype institution committed technical resources to begin designing and programming, while the permanent FCAAS staff was being assembled to eventually take over the system support. Funding was allocated to each of the prototype institutions to help replace resources that were lost while their systems were being developed. Together, these systems created a technical framework that allowed each of Florida's postsecondary institutions to transfer data and access information through FACTS.org. A five-year, multiphase function implementation plan was also developed for all participating institutions.

When the web site launched in 2000, it primarily offered postsecondary services. In 2001 the State Board of Education became the governing body for FCAAS, and the pendulum shifted to provide a more K–20 approach. Along with the legislature, it began to focus on meeting demands for postsecondary education, including expanding access and student preparedness. The web site was seen as a means to provide high school students from across the state with the ability to create a four-year high school planner that would prepare them for work, college, or a career.

High school and transfer services were then added to FACTS.org to complete the educational pipeline. There was a renewed focus on access issues, and efforts were made to provide mechanisms that could help students move more efficiently through secondary and postsecondary institutions. Building a statewide student advising system in house has been rewarding for Florida. The technology helps the state meet its specific needs and goals, including target graduation rates, preparedness for postsecondary education, accountability measures, and greater student achievement.

The web site receives about 13 million hits a year, with requests for college transcripts and degree audits topping the list. As FACTS.org becomes more integrated with campus business practices, schools are finding more and more ways to use the system and save their own resources. For example, a transient student form created for the system can automatically route a course request and registration between a home and transient institution, saving time for all parties concerned. Many institutions rely solely on FACTS.org as a grade distribution resource (foregoing mailing expenses); others opt to use its online admission applications in lieu of their own.

Again, the uniqueness of FACTS.org lies in its interconnectivity between institutions. Most institutions have their own web sites, but through FACTS.org we can provide those institutions with real-time evaluations.

Lessons Learned

Creating an online statewide student advising system from scratch is a challenging, yet rewarding, endeavor. Creating a system that provides real-time information to all users takes a strong commitment and years of effort. It also requires statewide articulation policies and resources. But when done with the support of leadership, the online system can be a tool that addresses the state's policy issues.

Andrea Latham is on the staff and Connie Graunke is the executive director of the Florida Department of Education, Florida Center for Advising and Academic Support, which designed and developed FACTS.

The other option that continues to pick up steam is outsourcing. These days, campuses contract for a wide variety of services, including the staging and hosting of official forms for admissions and housing; the collection of tuition payments and contributions; the ability to display grades, fulfill transcript requests, and provide transfer credit information; and career counseling.

Most of the time, the web interface is tailored to the institution's style, so the student is not aware that the service is coming from a third-party provider. By aggregating the needs of multiple-client institutions, corporate service providers can often deliver more robust and cost-effective service than colleges could provide in house.

The following essay describes how Broward Community College in Florida has strategically partnered with two vendors to provide high quality, scalable e-services.

Accelerating Your E-Service Initiatives Through Partnerships With Service Providers
Russ Adkins

Broward Community College (BCC), a large, multicampus institution located in south Florida, joined the e-learning movement in the late 1990s. BCC has been able to provide academic and student support services for its growing e-learning population by blending vendor-provided services with those provided by the institution. Vendor "partners" provide critically needed e-learning hosting and student help desk and instructional design services. They also augment on-the-ground tutoring services with "e-tutors."

Welcome to South Florida!
Not yet one month into my new job as Broward Community College's associate vice president for instructional technology, I learned that our health sciences provost was ready to announce a remarkable e-learning initiative. Her goal was to open access to BCC's nursing program to emergency medical technicians and other motivated persons whose jobs would not allow them to attend classes on campus. We would do this, she said, by putting the 10 "lecture" courses online, and providing a more flexible clinical schedule at area hospitals for the 30 nursing e-learning students we would begin admitting twice a year.

Perhaps this does not strike you as remarkable, but back in 1998, BCC did not have a single course online.

We Weren't Ready
We did have a course management system on a college server (sitting unused, for the most part). Our IT staff had little experience

supporting that application, which in those days was notoriously unstable. Instead, they were constantly up to their eyeballs trying to support another new application, or another migration. And, at that time, our help desk was limited to faculty and staff support, and only available Monday through Friday, 8 a.m. to 5 p.m.

The shaky ground extended beyond our technology infrastructure. There were also few resources to support faculty engaged in e-learning course development. We had no instructional designer to help instructors transform their campus-based courses.

I'd say that we weren't ready for e-learning.

Priorities and Partnerships

These barriers might have dissolved at an institution whose leader proclaimed e-learning to be mission critical, but our primary purpose at that time was more broadly focused on faculty development and less on the strategic application of technology and pedagogy to deliver degrees online.

To make a long story short, we entered into a partnership with a company called Eduprise (now called Sungard Higher Education). I call this relationship a partnership, because I frankly do not much care for the term "outsource." To me, outsourcing is sending jobs overseas, or taking a huge chunk of an enterprise and contracting another entity to run it. A partnership, on the other hand, is a relationship in which both entities help each other.

E-Learning Hosting and Help Desk Services

Our partner hosts all of our 900 e-learning course sections on its servers 210 miles north of our south Florida location. The partner's technical environment is inland and less vulnerable to the sort of catastrophic damage a hurricane can do to coastal areas. It also hosts our WebCT application and supports our 19,000 e-learning students with 24/7 help desk support. In the five years that the company has hosted our courses, the only service interruption we've had was caused by a database issue inside WebCT, and our partner worked hard and fast to fix it. As an added bonus, because our e-learning programs were externally hosted during Hurricanes Katrina and Wilma, our students and faculty had access to their e-learning courses in the immediate aftermath of Katrina and during the post-Wilma weeks that the college was closed.

Onsite E-Learning Instructional Design Services

Our agreement places a full-time instructional designer onsite. Funding for this aspect of the partnership has come from a series of federal grants that help BCC support healthcare workforce development initiatives using e-learning solutions. This doctoral-level professional adds value to all of our e-learning initiatives while being actively engaged in supporting the healthcare workforce (and of late, helping with bio-terrorism education for area healthcare agencies).

The Blend

The e-learning hosting, help desk, and instructional design services are blended into our local resources. We worked from the beginning to ensure that our partnership services complimented our local e-learning resources. As a result, our faculty and students regard all of the partnership services as though they were provided directly by Broward Community College. This suits the company just fine. After all, its job is to make us look good by providing services at the level of quality we need.

Students seamlessly follow a link off the college web site to "our" server at the company's location. Our instructional designer has a BCC email address and telephone number, and attends college meetings with the rest of us. He leads workshops and works with members of our e-learning team to support BCC's e-learning faculty.

E-Tutoring

Broward Community College more recently partnered with Smarthinking to provide students with more flexibility in accessing tutoring support. While the Sungard partnership is sharply focused on supporting students in e-learning classes, the Smarthinking relationship aims to be as useful for the campus-based learner as for the e-learner. This is consistent with other college efforts to better serve all BCC students with online registration, library, and advising services.

Until we partnered with Smarthinking, students could access tutoring services only by visiting a facility on one of our three primary campuses. Those tutoring services were limited to weekday work hours and early evenings, with spotty weekend hours. Even if students were able to find their way to a tutoring facility, the peer tutors on duty might not have expertise in the subject area they needed.

BCC engaged Smarthinking as one of several strategies to improve the overall effectiveness of tutoring. Student fees were modestly increased to fund these tutoring enhancements. Our students now have access to e-tutors during evenings and on weekends from any location where they can access the Internet. Students login to BCC's student web portal to use the service. After logging in, they can contact tutors with expertise in math, chemistry, biology, and accounting economics, as well as subjects for which we have limited campus-based services (English and Spanish essay-reading services and economics).

We know that Smarthinking's tutors are making a difference. Institutional research results indicate that students who receive tutoring through Smarthinking are more successful in their math and English courses than students who do not use Smarthinking (Anderson, 2005). Students who use Smarthinking tutoring services attain higher passing rates than their peers.

Now that we've demonstrated that students like e-tutoring, and are more successful as a result of using it, our tutoring team is preparing our "on-the-ground" tutors to provide tutoring support online. Our partner, Smarthinking, has given us access to its platform and is helping us prepare our existing tutors to move into the 21st century. Our tutoring team selected one of our most popular tutors to provide online support in chemistry and mathematics during times that BCC's on-the-ground tutoring facility is closed.

Following the precedent set by our interaction with Sungard Higher Education, we are now blending Smarthinking-provided services with local resources to improve the overall quality of tutoring for our students.

Scale and Economies of Scale

The partnerships described in this chapter may not be appropriate for your institution. BCC was able to implement e-learning hosting and help desk services (and more recently, e-tutoring services) within a matter of months. We did not have to buy equipment that we would later have to refresh, upgrade, or repair, and we did not have to recruit, hire, train, or replace staff.

Sure, these services cost us money. But the financial hit is softened by two primary factors:

- Our partner helps us achieve an economy of scale, because its cost is shared among a number of clients.

- We can spread the cost of service across a large number of students. By way of example, a student e-learning fee of $4 per credit hour (typically $12 per 3-credit course) offsets our Sungard hosting and help desk expenses and pays our learning management system license fee.

Perhaps the most elegant consequence of both partnerships is that we will continue to grow, and the cost of our growth is predictable. Contracts have been written to ensure that our partners are prepared to absorb our growth while maintaining service quality.

Advice to Those Interested in Partnering to Support e-Services

Any partnership has risks, but these can be reduced by carefully defining your service expectations—at the beginning and in the midterm—with measurable outcomes. Ensure that your partnership agreement anticipates growth and that services can be scaled to accommodate your success.

Always structure your agreements in such a way that you can withdraw, if necessary. Avoid getting into a partnership that would make it impossible to change vendors or bring the services back to campus.

Russ Adkins is <u>associate vice president for instructional technology</u> at Broward Community College, FL. To find out more about Broward's technology initiatives, see www.broward.edu/itech

Benchmarking Your Online Services and Learning From Best Practices

The web has made the operations of colleges and universities more public than ever before. Is it any wonder, then, that administrators are becoming increasingly concerned about the type of services they offer online?

To help institutions set benchmarks and to build awareness about best practices, Pat Shea and Darlene Burnett—in partnership with the Minnesota State Colleges and University System (MnSCU)—developed an audit tool. This tool currently focuses on 20 student services: academic advising, admissions, assessment and testing, the bookstore, career planning, the course catalog, communications (from the institution to the student), financial aid, the library, orientation, registration, personal counseling, placement services, scheduling of classes, services for international students, services for students with disabilities, student accounts, student activities, technical support, and tutoring.

With assistance from experts in each area, the researchers identified critical components for each service, whether delivered face to face or in an online environment. In career counseling, for example, students may want to make an appointment with a counselor, take an interest assessment, explore careers relating to a major, or find a job. Altogether, the researchers identified more than 160 critical components across the 20 services.

For each critical component, there are descriptions for four levels of service, based on an expanded version of Darlene Burnett's model of four generations of web service. In this model, Generation One is brochure-ware. Institutions take what they have in print and put it on the web. Generation Two services focus on groups of students, offering different paths for different kinds of students and providing one-way communication through online and email forms. On the home page, there are options for prospective, transfer, current, and distance students, and information throughout the site is organized that way for them. In Generation Three, students can login to portals where information and services are personalized and customized individually for them. Usually there are multiple portals with different IDs and/or passwords, including one for the library, another for career counseling, and another for academic advising. Generation Four features high-tech, high-touch services, using smart technologies to anticipate and deliver just-in-time assistance. By simply logging in to the institution's portal, a student can access all services, although Generation Four services may also exist on the public site outside the portal.

Let's look at an example of one critical component for career counseling from the audit tool: "As a student, I can make an appointment with a career counselor." By selecting the description that most aptly matches the service your campus offers, you can benchmark your campus's service for this component at one of the following levels.

- *Generation Zero.* Students can find no information about making an appointment with a career counselor.

- *Generation One.* Students can find an office location and a telephone number for scheduling appointments.

- *Generation Two.* Students can click on a counselor's email address to contact him or her about requesting an appointment.

- *Generation Three.* Students can view a counselor's calendar online and schedule an appointment for one of the available times.

- *Generation Four.* Students can cross-reference their calendar, and their reasons for needing an appointment, with a counselor's calendar to find a selection of convenient appointment openings. They can then select and schedule the appointment, along with a request for a reminder to be sent 24 hours in advance, with appropriate preparation material.

To expand the availability of the audit tool and this research in best practices in online student services, WCET—in partnership with MnSCU and Seward Inc., a leader in the design and development of custom e-learning software and e-business solutions—launched the Center for Transforming Student Services (CENTSS; see www.centss.org) in November 2005.

CENTSS is a virtual resource for higher education institutions interested in assessing the quality of their online student services. Of primary importance among the center's resources is the CENTSS Online Audit Tool, which institutions can license to assess their online student services or contract for an assessment by a CENTSS expert. A confidential report helps institutions identify their strengths and weaknesses. Using collected data from participating institutions, CENTSS issues an annual report that provides the institutions with a basis for comparing their services to those of the competition.

Even at this stage, the audit tool is pointing out the need for institutional leaders to take a stronger interest in their web presence. A key finding is that many administrators and staff members do not know what is on their web site, and it is unclear whose responsibility it is to keep the information up to date. In the defense of student services staff, they sometimes have a different view of their campus services behind the firewall than that of the students they serve, so it is difficult for them to know how to best help students or improve their web pages.

Just how bad is it? At one audited institution, we could find no office hours for academic advisors. We thought it was an oversight, but it turned out that the staff in the advising department did not want to be tied down to any specific hours. This was a big surprise to the top administrators. Another institution offered students the opportunity to start classes on a flexible schedule throughout the year, something that would have been very attractive to many students *if* it had been mentioned anywhere on the web site.

How much does this matter? A lot! If you have ever watched a modern-day high school or college student surf the web, you know how fast they decide that a site is not helpful and click on another one. In fact, one study found that visitors to a web site make a decision to move on based on the aesthetic appearance of the site in less time than it takes to blink an eye. In this increasingly competitive higher education environment, can your institution afford to let that happen?

Summing Up

The web offers institutions a unique opportunity to provide better and more accessible service to all students, whether they attend class on campus or not. Thanks to new technology, campuses can deliver student-centered services with the characteristics those students have come to expect: self-service, just-in-time, personalized, customized, customizable, interactive, integrated, and consistent. Models integrated with the web—including one-stop center and program-level services—offer new promise in serving and retaining students. Other web services designed for specific segments of the student population, such as transfer or distance students, can help those students get acclimated more quickly. These days, campuses are increasingly looking for ways to outsource or collaborate in the delivery of web services. Now institutions can look to the Center for Transforming Student Services for resources and best practices research.

Endnote

1) The "Guidelines for Creating Student Services Online" were published by WCET in its Learning Anytime Anywhere Partnership
   project, "Beyond the Administrative Core: Creating Web-Based
   Services for Online Learners."

Reference

Anderson, P. (2005). *Does tutoring help? A comparison of SmartThinking
tutored and non-tutored students' grades and college-wide 2005.* Fort
Lauderdale, FL: Broward Community College.

Shea, P., & Armitage, S. (2003). *Guidelines for creating student services
online.* Retrieved July 19, 2006, from the WCET web site:
www.wcet.info/projects/laap/guidelines/index.asp

*Patricia (Pat) Shea is assistant director for WCET, with oversight for the
annual conference and the membership program. She also heads WCET's
research efforts in online student services via the new Center for
Transforming Student Services (CENTSS). She is a codeveloper of the Audit
Tool used by institutions to identify strengths and weaknesses in their online
student services. She also provides consulting services to institutions and consortia on designing or improving their web-based student services. Shea sits
on the board of the Fulbright Association's Colorado Chapter.*

4 ··· How Can We Help the Faculty?

Sally M. Johnstone

Any teacher that can be replaced by a computer deserves to be.

—Robert Maynard Hutchins (1899–1977),
President of the University of Chicago (1929–1951)

There are many implications in Hutchins's pronouncement that lead one to think hard about how we are using online tools and how faculty are dealing with them. In a recent article (Silverstein, 2006) in the *Los Angeles Times*, faculty members at a number of higher education institutions complained that when they posted their class lectures online, fewer students came to class. Around the time that article appeared, Apple Computer announced it would allow any college or university to set up its own customized section of the iTunes Music Store to allow them to distribute course materials and other unique audio or video materials (Young, 2006). Apple piloted this concept with six high-profile institutions during the previous year, and everyone seemed pretty satisfied. The students especially appreciated the ability to have a mobile system to review materials while they walked across campus, worked out, or flipped burgers at their part-time job.

I do not mean to take the faculty's concerns lightly. After all, the teaching part of their jobs has traditionally involved lecturing to their students, answering their questions, coaching them, and assessing them. It is what our current faculty experienced when they went to college, and it is what the parents of our students expect their children to experience. But now that students have access to electronic versions of class materials, they are better able to maximize their class time to get a reasonable grade. Students have always done this. They have borrowed notes from one another, exchanged information about which classes would cover material on which they would be examined, used class times to sleep, and so on. These types of behaviors are not new.

What *is* new is the reality that there are a variety of ways, besides sitting in a classroom, students can get the information they need to become proficient in a subject area. As I mentioned in Chapter 1, the leaders on many campuses are discovering that half of the students taking online or distance education courses were actually on the campus that offered the online course. Not only are thousands of students taking fully online courses from traditional institutions, tens of thousands more are using online course management systems that open access to academic materials beyond the classroom. At about half of our campuses across the county, when a faculty member is approved to teach a new course, he or she is assigned a web site for that class. Green's 2005 Campus Computing Survey indicated that approximately 50% of public and private universities and four-year colleges in the U.S. had course management systems available to all faculty members on the campus. The rate for community colleges was a little more than 30% (see www.campuscomputing.net). Over the last few years, as most colleges and universities have switched their distance learning course offerings from video to an online format, administrators have found that a lot of the growth in online classes is due to on-campus students.

Students' desire to take advantage of online learning opportunities is probably motivated by several factors. Today's students are more likely to be working full- or part-time jobs than students in the past. As a result, their schedules are constrained. In any given semester they may need a particular class that is not offered on campus or that does not have any seats available on campus. For some students, it may be that the online version of a course offers a better learning opportunity. Whatever the reason, it is important to note that this is happening and that it has a profound effect on what faculty members do in their role as teachers.

Since students want more learning options and most campus managers want to attract more students, it makes sense to offer students these options. As discussed in Chapter 2, few campuses could afford to do this if the technological options were simply added on to what was already being done by the faculty. It would create a situation in which the expenses that were always there remained, but with added operating costs. When campuses add wireless networks to classrooms, some faculty are seriously troubled, especially if students sit in class and check their email or instant message their friends. (Or worse—if they explore information sources that are more recent than those being used by the faculty member.) Simply adding a wireless network does not help faculty members, although network access may give students more reasons to sit in the classroom.

Faculty members who post their lecture notes online can use class time for activities that cannot be captured in notes. They may choose to meet with students in smaller groups for a couple of hours each week, rather than all at once for 50 minutes, three times a week. These teachers may be ready to toss off traditional roles in favor of using more sophisticated course materials that students can work through on their own. This frees the teachers to spend more time with the students who really need help. I will share some interesting examples.

A few years ago at Virginia Tech, the engineering faculty discovered that the course in which first-year students were most likely to perform poorly was linear algebra. Their poor performance in this course seemed to be the biggest single reason that students were dropping out of engineering studies. While the faculty could have blamed faulty preparation, they chose instead to turn these poor performances around by completely redesigning the course. To manage all of this, Virginia Tech's math faculty created a Math Emporium housed in an old department store on the edge of the campus.

Virginia Tech's Math Emporium
Anne H. Moore

The Math Emporium is a 500-workstation advanced learning community in mathematics, staffed by faculty, teaching assistants, and undergraduate peer tutors who provide one-on-one assistance for more than 20 courses. Since it opened in 1997, the emporium has served as a site for advancing technology-assisted approaches to teaching and learning, with frequent assessments of student performance and of faculty roles and attitudes. In developing courses for the emporium, math faculty may choose from existing texts, software, or tutorials to develop an appropriate approach to technology-assisted instruction.

Linear algebra was the first course in the emporium that was totally redesigned by the math faculty, from text and tutorials to quizzes and tests. The redesign replaced the 40-student multiple section model with one large course structure. A web-based resource system that consisted of interactive tutorials, computation examples, an electronic textbook, and online quizzes increased student feedback and facilitated 24/7 access to course materials.

The redesign of linear algebra has reduced the cost-per-student for this course from $77 to $24, resulting in a projected annual operating cost savings of $97,400. The associated faculty resources have been redirected to advanced mathematics courses where smaller, more intimate student-faculty interaction is required.

The university's Office of Institutional Research and Planning Analysis conducted a statistical analysis of the project's effectiveness. The analysis, issued in March 1999, found that "those students who receive their math instruction via the Math Emporium exhibit improved performance" (Muffo & Taylor, 1999). External evaluators of the project were quite impressed.

The University of Idaho and the University of Alabama are replicating the basic design of the Math Emporium with very different student populations. As Mike Williams, Virginia Tech's Math Emporium director, puts it, "In a nutshell, the lectures for large enrollment, introductory courses were not proving a very effective approach to learning mathematics. We wanted to develop a different model where, instead of broadcasting one to many, we changed it to more of a one-on-one tutorial."

Anne H. Moore is associate vice president for learning technologies at Virginia Tech.

Virginia Tech's Math Emporium is a great example of how creative faculty members can use information and communication technologies to create a better learning environment that actually costs less than the traditional way of teaching. It took strong leaders to insist that the academic staff at the institution find ways to help students be more successful. But when challenged to step outside of their usual way of doing things, teachers who love their subject area can achieve remarkable results.

There are dozens of similar examples of faculty using technology for course redesign (for example, see Chapter 2 for a description of the National Center for Academic Transformation's Program in Course Redesign [Twigg, 2003]).

Faculty Transitions: The Big Picture

It is important to note that not all faculty members are comfortable with such an intensive use of technology. Traditional teaching is a solitary activity; faculty members adopt a textbook, create lectures and other class-based exercises, offer these to the students, and assess the students' learning. Several years ago, Dennis Jones, president of the National Center for Higher Education Management Systems (NCHEMS; see www.nchems.org), and I cochaired a working group for a federally supported organization that examined the effect technology had on national data collection. As part of that work, our group developed a way of describing how the tasks associated with teaching and supporting students' learning were becoming unbundled. This set of tasks was used in

WCET's Technology Costing Methodology tools described in Chapter 2. We characterized those tasks as:

- Curriculum development

- Content development

- Information delivery

- Mediation/tutoring

- Student support services

- Administration

- Assessment

This list represents the traditional tasks of academic employees in higher education. Several of them have already been unbundled. We already have specialists within our colleges and universities who focus exclusively on administration and student support services. While many of these individuals may have started their careers as faculty members, they now have their own unique professional world. As electronic technologies become integrated into the collegiate experience, there are more and more opportunities for businesses to assist higher education in these unbundled tasks. Thanks to electronic links, the location of the provider of these services becomes less relevant, and each task need not be completely replicated on every campus. Consequently, colleges and universities can join together to form a sufficient base of users to make the development of new, high-quality electronic services feasible (see Chapter 6).

Another way to consider the importance of well-designed course materials is to look at shifts in the use of full-time faculty for teaching. According to the Southern Regional Education Board (2005), during the 2003–2004 school year, institutions crossed over the 50% point for full- versus part-time faculty teaching U.S. students. In four-year institutions, more than 55% of the teaching staff is part-time or is made up of teaching and research assistants. At community colleges, part-timers represent almost 68% of the teaching staff. This trend toward reducing the number of full-time faculty raises many issues. One is that we are already well down the path of unbundling the faculty role. There is also a need for academic leaders to pay close attention to ensuring the consistent quality of students' learning experiences. At many colleges and universities, a common textbook is used as a primary guarantee of consistency. This may not be sufficient for either consistency or quality, especially as economic models push us toward serving larger numbers of students with fewer resources.

As Michael Goldstein points out in his essay in Chapter 1, many of the proprietary postsecondary institutions that have developed in the last several years use a very different model for teaching staff. This is a model that is also popular with open universities around the world, which serve hundreds of thousands of students and do so at a reasonable cost (Daniel, 1996). They employ nonteaching faculty members to be part of teams that develop course materials for students. Then the teaching faculty use those materials and are free to personalize classes (whether online or face to face) based on their own special knowledge. The new institutions that follow this model have the advantage of designing a teaching staff system from scratch to fit current realities. More traditional institutions are trying to retrofit a new system onto one that no longer seems affordable.

It is a challenge to move from traditional practices and policies into this new way of doing things. Colleges and universities cannot afford to ignore this challenge. The students that are coming to our campuses are expecting their college experience to fit the learning styles to which they have become accustomed. You can find more ideas about serving these digital natives in the Chapter 7, but in order to serve them well, we must first shift the way we think about teaching and learning.

Institutional Policies for New Faculty Models

When clever people are given new tools, they figure out how to use them—and university and college faculty members and their students are some of the most clever people around. As they develop new ways to work together, institutional leaders need to examine policies and practices that may be barriers to new ways of doing things, because they were developed in an earlier era. With good reason, colleges and universities, states, and the federal government have established a set of policies that protects students and funding sources from bad and fraudulent practices. These policies were initially developed to fit a culture that did not include online teaching and learning tools. Now that we have these new tools and are beginning to discover their power to enhance learning, we need to revise our former methods.

As previously mentioned, colleges and universities are trying to offer better service to more students (and doing so with fewer resources), which is changing the way course materials are being developed and used. This is part of the reason there are more adjunct and part-time faculty members working directly with students. But this also sets up some potential conflict with quality assurance agencies, as they may question the practice of using a large proportion of adjunct faculty. If we are going to fully utilize the power of technological tools for teaching, we must move beyond the unitary model of what constitutes a faculty member. Not all individuals who serve as members of faculties have the same skills and responsibilities. We can no longer act as if the most important function of a full-time, promotable faculty member is his or her ability to get research articles published and serve on campus committees. I do not want to suggest that generating new knowledge is not an important academic function for universities, but I do question the efficacy of using the same standards for all members of the teaching workforce. Our inability to sort out this issue has led to the recent involvement of the United Auto Workers (UAW), which represents adjunct faculty members at New York University. Huge groups of university teaching assistants are also organizing into unions. Graduate student employee groups are affiliating with UAW and with the more traditional faculty unions, the American Federation of Teachers (AFT) and the National Education Association (NEA). At the last joint meeting of the AFT and the NEA, the sessions on issues for adjunct faculty members were some of the best attended (Jaschik, 2006). All of this suggests we have some real problems with our traditional policies and practices regarding the treatment of the teaching workforce.

Faculty and Course Materials

As noted, one strategy for ensuring the coherence of the curriculum and the quality of specific courses is to use teams of faculty to develop course materials, which are then administered by others who work directly with students. The Open University in the U.K. has used this strategy for several decades. It began by offering complete courses in print coupled with broadcast video, then connected students to tutors who helped them work through the course materials. The Open University has gone on to develop quite sophisticated technology-enhanced course materials, but the basic mechanism is the same: Thousands of students use one set of materials while groups of tutors work directly with them—either face to face or online. This model is used successfully by open universities around the world. Back in the U.S., there is a very interesting project to which I want to draw your attention. In 2002 Carnegie Mellon University (CMU) launched a new set of electronic course materials for use by higher education institutions that was an outgrowth of CMU's well-known cognitive science research activities. All of the electronic learning environments developed by CMU for use by other institutions incorporate cognitive tutors, virtual laboratories, group experiments, and simulations, and can be delivered completely online—as replacements for textbooks, in combination with recitation sections, or as supplements to traditional instructor-led courses. This collection, which includes subjects like statistics, chemistry, logic, biology, economics, physics, and even French, was originally developed for local students. However, thanks to support from the William and Flora Hewlett Foundation, it has evolved into the CMU Open Learning Initiative. The following essay shows us what faculty members can do in this type of teaching environment.

....

Open Learning Initiatives at Carnegie Mellon University
Candace Thille and Joel Smith

Faculty at Carnegie Mellon University and other institutions are using web-based learning environments developed through the Open Learning Initiative (OLI; see www.cmu.edu/oli) to address many of the challenges involved in teaching introductory college courses effectively.

Novice learners in a new domain have the greatest need for teaching practices that foster robust learning: individualized instruction, targeted and timely feedback, an explicit conceptual framework for organizing new knowledge, and interactive learning activities that support students, helping them practice new skills and make connections between related skills and concepts. Unfortunately, growing enrollment brings with it a growing variability in students' prior knowledge and skills in introductory courses, making it difficult and costly for institutions to employ such practices and address diverse student needs. As a result, students often end up memorizing isolated facts and procedures or focusing on typical textbook problems. Many perform well on traditional exams, but are unable to apply their knowledge to novel problems or future courses. This is an area in which contemporary information technology—informed by the learning sciences—can make a difference.

The Open Learning Initiative creates web-based learning environments that support the novice learner, based on the best current research from the learning and cognitive sciences. Teams of faculty content experts, cognitive and learning scientists, and specialists in

human computer interaction collaborate to create, evaluate, and
iteratively improve OLI courses. As students move through these
courses, the system collects information about their performance.
This information is later used to provide them with feedback and
helps course developers make further improvements to the course.
Evaluative studies have confirmed the effectiveness of the OLI
learning environments in supporting individual novice learners.

The project has recently turned its attention to investigating
how the same information about student performance that provides
meaningful feedback to course designers can also be given to course
instructors to support them in effectively adapting their lessons.
One of the great assets of e-learning environments is their unique
ability to simultaneously deliver instruction while gathering data on
what is and is not working to support student learning. We are now
developing tools that combine different areas in the OLI courses to
provide instructors with real-time feedback about their students'
progress. This feedback goes far beyond "pages visited" or "assessments taken." It is very rich information that provides instructors
with a summary view of their students' comprehension levels and
helps them drill down to the details of individual student work.
With this feedback, instructors can review the areas students find
difficult, clarify connections among different concepts, assign additional work, or move on to another topic.

In fall 2005 we began to test the following hypothesis: If the
professor of a large lecture course uses our system to customize
instruction to his or her students' needs, the students' learning will
surpass levels found in traditional lecture environments.

We conducted a five-week study with two sections (Section A
and Section B) of the Carnegie Mellon Modern Biology course,
which comprised more than 300 students. In week one, both sections had access to the same introductory material in their lectures
and online course. In weeks two and three, Section A continued to
use the online course and attended one large class discussion per

week, but did not attend three traditional lecture sessions. The course instructor asked students in Section A to complete specific modules of the online course by Sunday evening, so that before the weekly class meeting on Monday, he could look over the feedback reports from the online system and adapt his instruction accordingly. During this two-week period, Section B did not have access to the online course; instead, the instructor covered the same material in three weekly lectures. During weeks four and five, the sections reversed roles—Section B used the online course, while Section A no longer had access to the online course and began attending the weekly lectures. At the end of week five, all students took the same midterm.

A challenge we confronted during the study illustrates students' feelings about the value of the online material: Students in Section A (the first online group) registered for Section B's online course after their access to the online material had been terminated. To maintain the integrity of the study, we had to remove or block students who were in Section A from further using these materials.

Although there were many noteworthy results, these are among the key findings:

- Observations of the two sections revealed that students were more active in class discussions when they were using the online course.

- An exam given at the end of the third week revealed that those using the online materials had a distinct advantage.

- Detailed analyses of data logs showed a positive and significant association between the time students spent working on particular online activities and their performance on related quiz questions (Lovett, 2006).

The Open Learning Initiative courses represent the "textbook of the future" in the range of learning support tools they provide and their capacity to give instructors meaningful feedback on student learning. These e-learning tools will someday be as essential to knowledge transfer as printed texts have been for the past few hundred years. They are, in the best sense, a "disruptive technology" that could significantly transform the way we conceive of teaching and learning. Although the learning sciences have reported for years that frequent, immediate, meaningful, context-sensitive, learner-centered feedback is critical to improving teaching and learning, the cost of providing such feedback (using only human capital) has previously been prohibitive. If online textbooks that emulate the style of Open Learning Initiative courses are used by instructors to provide this kind of feedback, then the nature of what instructors do with face-to-face time can finally change. This time could be used for more complex activities—motivating, mentoring, engaging in dialogue or collaborative exploration, and community building—activities that are usually deferred, because the classroom, so dependent on printed texts, has been considered the only place for meaningful feedback. The Open Learning Initiative approach is changing that story.

Candace Thille is director of the Open Learning Initiative, and Joel Smith vice provost and chief information officer for computing services at Carnegie Mellon University.

Course Importers

In Chapter 6 we take a closer look at how faculty members are beginning to share course materials. The previous CMU example shows how much can be gained when teachers work together to create materials, but it begs the question of who, other than those involved in creating the materials, will use them. The CMU courses are being used by dozens of colleges and high schools. There are also state-level course importers. Recently, the state of West Virginia contracted with the state of Kentucky to deliver online courses to their remote students. Instructors in the Kentucky colleges were already working in an online teaching environment, and the West Virginia higher education planners realized they could serve their limited number of online students more cost effectively by paying for the service instead of investing in extra personnel, software, and infrastructure development.

There are also intrastate approaches to course importing. Some states even encourage their institutions to share electronically delivered courses. The South Dakota Board of Regents decided not to fund competitive electronically delivered courses at state institutions. Instead, it was expected that campuses would share their online programs. Similarly, in April 2003 the Nebraska Coordinating Commission for Postsecondary Education passed a resolution that actually promoted inter-institutional sharing of courses through the use of instructional technology and cross-registration. Of course, it is important to note that both of these decisions were driven by the economic pressures placed on rural states. Not all faculties will be as willing to use course materials they did not create.

Through an unpuplished 2003 WCET survey conducted as part of the Hewlett Foundation project, we discovered that not all institutions are quite ready to consider importing courses from another institution or commercial provider. Just 12 of the 48 institutions we surveyed said that their faculty and staff would prefer online course materials developed elsewhere. Yet most of the staff members interviewed indicated that they were interested in making their institution's courses available to others. It is interesting to note that the reasons given for preferring courses developed in house included the need to focus on local students and a general faculty preference for using their own courses. In some cases, faculty preference was presented as a positive factor; in others, as a negative one. In several cases, the faculty's "not-developed-here" culture was considered a restraint on activities that might otherwise be positive for the institution.

What we are finding now is that commercially developed online courses are being more widely used at the high school level than at higher education institutions. This is mostly due to a lack of qualified teachers in specific fields who can serve students in smaller school districts. Some higher education institutions are beginning to experience the same problem. Chapter 6 provides examples of consortia that share courses at colleges and universities because they cannot afford or find faculty to offer courses that students need to complete some of their on-campus degree programs. This is a problem that is not expected to go away. As a result, there are some faculty issues that must be resolved before they become impediments to faculty collaboration. One such issue concerns the ownership of academic materials and shared resources.

Intellectual Property

As we start to consider some of the issues around faculty members and their creation of intellectual property, it may be useful to remember that moral rights are distinct and separate from the economic rights embodied in a copyright (R. McCracken, personal communication, March, 2006). In several countries these "moral rights" are part of the legal system. That is not the case in the U.S., but it is certainly assumed by most creators of academic materials. As you will see in several examples that follow, it is useful to distinguish between these concepts when determining the rights of an institution and the rights of a faculty member over materials created as part of the faculty member's teaching load. In the U.S., the closest thing we have to moral rights are what are usually referred to as "rights of use."

When we move into a mostly or entirely online teaching situation, there may be problems with our traditional model. It may not work as well to have a single faculty member develop and manage a course for a small number of students. As we have already seen, it is usually more cost effective if a team—made up of faculty members, instructional designers, technology experts, editors, and others—develops the course materials. It also tends to guarantee a better quality product. Those who manage the students as they work through these course materials may not be the same people who created the materials. A question then arises about the intellectual ownership of the course materials.

When only one faculty member is used as the subject matter expert in the development process, many campuses grant the intellectual property rights to that individual—with caveats. The caveats frequently include the right of the campus to use the materials in perpetuity, but allow the faculty member the opportunity to review and potentially revise the materials on a regular basis. Naturally, the time between revisions may be a function of the subject itself. A course on tax codes will need to be revised annually, but an art history course is likely to have a longer shelf life. Course materials can also be structured to allow for revisions of the particular sections that are likely to change over time. Whatever the case, a three-year review process is not unusual.

Another caveat that smart institutional leaders build into their contracts with faculty members involves *where* instructors may use these teaching materials. If a faculty member uses institutional resources to create online materials for a course, then the institution needs to safeguard its investment. The agreement between the faculty member and the institution could bar that person from taking the online product to another institution to teach. The faculty member could take his or her intellectual knowledge, but would have to use the new institution's resources to create a new product.

IP Policy Examples

There are many approaches to sorting out intellectual property issues for faculty and their institutions, and no single model will work for every situation. WCET's EduTools (see www.edutools.info) project has collected dozens of college and university intellectual property policies. These can be viewed by anyone.

The policy at Arkansas Tech University is a fairly straightforward example of online course ownership:

> When the University contracts with an employee for the development of a specific online course or other distance learning product, it will be considered a work made for hire for a period of two years from the date the course is first offered. Two years after the course has been developed, and upon approval of the Vice President for Academic Affairs, the course can also be used by the employee who developed it, for other teaching, research, and scholarly purposes.
>
> A totally faculty or staff generated online course that has received no direct support from Arkansas Tech and without the use of any Arkansas Tech resources beyond those normally provided will remain the property of the developer. (EduTools, 2006a, ¶s 1–2)

Many institutions have incorporated the development of online teaching materials into their traditional intellectual property agreements. This usually involves differentiating among the institutional resources that are used in the creation of the materials, or "creative works." If few college or university resources are used in the creative work, then the intellectual property or product remains in the total control of the creator. However, when substantial college or university resources are used in the production of creative works, the institution typically retains its ownership position, and simply shares income from the project with its developers. It is also not uncommon for the project's faculty author to reserve the (moral) right to periodically review the material for possible revisions. The period of review is usually determined by several factors, including the cost of revising the course.

The rights of use for intellectual property can appear quite simple, yet still cover the most common circumstances, as is the case with the University of Wisconsin System:

Where the Board of Regents, on behalf of the UW System or a UW institution, owns a copyright interest in instructional materials, the materials should receive timely and periodic review by users and producers to insure currency and relevance, consistent with the following:

Copyrightable instructional materials shall not be altered or revised without consultation with the author.

If the producing institution continues the use of copyrightable materials, or authorizes the use of such materials by others, contrary to the recommendation of the author, the producing institution shall not advertise or present the materials as the work of that author, except to the extent appropriate to acknowledge the author's participation in the original production of the copyrightable materials. (EduTools, 2006b, ¶s 9–11)

The most important part of a policy on intellectual property is to have one!

Everyone should know what the policy is before any online materials are created. Administrators in the early days of electronic materials development rarely had policies in place. These pioneers found themselves negotiating different deals with each faculty member who developed electronic course materials. This resulted in major recordkeeping nightmares and a lot of unhappy, dissatisfied faculty members (except the ones who got the best deals).

The best resource I have found on sorting out intellectual property issues is a crash course on copyright law, created by Georgia Harper (2001), the manager of the Intellectual Property Section of the Office of General Counsel for the University of Texas System. While it does not solve all of the sticky policy conundrums, it does spell out what you need to know when creating online learning materials. As Harper points out, the usual fair use issues, as applied to a classroom, are not so simple in cyberspace. The University of Texas has created a set of guidelines for course material developers to use, but the school points out that if there is any doubt, the developer should get permission to use the materials. Harper's crash course on copyright site takes users through a series of steps to determine the ownership of intellectual materials.

Importance of Disseminating IP Policies

Most colleges and universities are at the stage where almost all of their faculty and students are using online materials for class assignments. It is critical for all of the members of these campus communities to understand what they legally can and cannot do. Without a strong educational program and guidelines on appropriate use of online materials, campuses may find themselves paying lawyers a lot of money, which is rarely a good idea when you are trying to be more efficient with the use of your resources.

It is important for campus leaders to consider the following admonition from the Open University's head of intellectual property, Richard McCraken (personal communication, March, 2006): "Online, the license totally defines the product: what and how much content may be accessed; for how long; what can be done with it and the kind of services and support a user will receive. Definitions matter. They are what you deliver." When we have a book, we know what we can do with it—we can read it ourselves, then pass it along to another person. With electronic materials, the rules are not so clear. Despite many national and international efforts, we do not yet have commonly agreed upon ways of dealing with electronic information. As the whole file-sharing phenomenon of Napster and others has shown us, we need to pay close attention to how electronic information such as course materials, music, and films is used by campus communities. The courts will be further defining the parameters of electronic rights for many years to come. It is important to stay aware as things change.

Creative Commons

A relatively new approach to intellectual property for online materials was devised by Creative Commons (see www.creativecommons.org). This nonprofit organization was founded by Stanford Law Professor Lawrence Lessig, a national authority on intellectual property law. Creative Commons seeks to rebuild a healthy public domain by offering creators legal and technical tools for their works. Creative Commons licenses enable authors to retain their copyrights while allowing certain uses:

- *Attribution.* Anyone can use the posted material, but it must be attributed to the original author.

- *No commercial use.* The material is available for educational or personal use, but if anyone wants to create a commercial product, that person must negotiate with the original author.

- *No derivative works.* Anyone can use the posted material, but it cannot be used as a basis for creating new things.

- *Share alike.* People who create derivative content have to release it under this license so others can use it.

Creative Commons has built on the "all rights reserved" traditional copyright to create a voluntary "some rights reserved" copyright. This seems to be a comfortable option for faculty who would like to share their intellectual, teaching-related endeavors. Creative Commons' first project was launched in December 2002; by the end of 2005, there were more than 50 million licenses on the Creative Commons site, which speaks to the vital need for these intellectual options. The organization is run as a free, open resource to anyone who wants to open up their web-based content to the world. It is helping make the web a richer educational resource for everyone.

Creating a New Vision for Faculty Roles

In 2004 WCET staff pulled together a group of people to explore some of the issues faculty members face when they use technology to serve students on and off campus. (The panel included Thomas Duffy, Antoine Garibaldi, Mildred Garcia, Michele Haney, Nitza Hernandez, Katrina Meyer, Eugene Rice, and WCET staff members—Sharmila Basu Conger, Sally Johnstone, Russell Poulin, and Patricia Shea). We began the project, which was supported by the Lumina Foundation, with the premise that technology is a transformative tool. Our panel then discussed shifts in the academic culture and addressed the issue of an overloaded faculty by imagining a learner-centered, technology-aided academy. In this vision, the definition of faculty would be so changed that teams of individuals—including everyone that served students within the academy—would work to provide the most exceptional learning environment possible.

We developed the following categories to represent many of the issues facing faculty members in today's colleges and universities. Many of these issues involve topics previously covered in this chapter.[1]

A New Academic Culture

We are in the midst of a critical shift in higher education. A generation of faculty is retiring, and the new generation that is replacing them has fundamentally different ideas, ideals, and views on what it means to serve an institution. The new generation is a "we" generation, one that eschews traditional faculty isolation for the pleasure of working in teams and creating cross-disciplinary collaborations with industry profession-als as well as other academics. This generation wants to share the responsibility and the credit for their achievements in research and teaching.

An "Unworkable" Workload

In the midst of this cultural shift—and in the absence of a policy shift—it is not surprising that faculty members are becoming more and more overloaded. Instead of rewarding the "we" behavior that results from the cultural shift, institutions often continue to reward faculty with tenure and salary increases for demonstrating what they can achieve by themselves. As a result, those faculty who want to explore collaborative research, teaching, or online course development options end up having to do so in addition to the individual work that reaps formal rewards. As new faculty members enter the academy and are mentored by experienced faculty, this unspoken agreement to take on additional responsibilities ends up being passed from one generation to the next.

The Absence of Professional Development

Another barrier faced by faculty members is the idea that a professor's duties should remain constant throughout his or her career. Traditionally, faculty members must become tenured to secure their position, but they generally continue to do most of the same things (research, teaching, writing, and administration) before and after they receive tenure. Each of these things is important, but in light of time and energy constraints, faculty members may be better off focusing on specific areas at different moments in their careers, with experienced faculty serving as mentors for each shift.

If we really want to improve learning outcomes for our students, we need to improve teaching. And to improve teaching, we need to rethink the way faculty members fit in today's institutions. As faculty members are inexorably drawn into the new academic culture, the shift (though painful at the moment) could ultimately result in a transformative experience for the academy. With this in mind, our faculty identified several methods for easing the transition. Faculty members with whom we spoke pointed out that it is crucial to get institutional leadership involved in the process of rethinking the policies of higher education. Teachers must be encouraged to focus on the scholarship of teaching and learning in a way that makes sense for their subject matter and fits into an accepted reward structure.

Before institutional leaders begin the transformation process toward a new academic culture, they need to ask themselves the following questions:

- What policy changes can enable their institutions to embrace the shift in academic culture and reward faculty appropriately?

- What new kinds of faculty development processes are needed?

- How do they encourage the development of traits that are necessary to teach effectively in an ICT-rich environment?

- What strategies do they already have or need to have to encourage faculty to embrace new roles?

Institutions don't seem to reward faculty members for adding the development of online courses (hopefully as part of a team) or the scholarship of teaching and learning to their already overflowing plates. Is it possible to accomplish new educational goals without overloading faculty? Moving to a more team-centered approach could help. Teams could include (but not be limited to) academic deans, course developers, content experts, instructors, librarians, and student support personnel. These teams could incorporate ICTs into their course development and delivery strategies while designing appropriate student support systems to encourage persistence and collaborating with each other across institutions. This may sound ambitious, but there are several institutions already working this way, including Rio Salado College and the University of Phoenix (both in Arizona) and Touro International University (in California).

To get these types of transformation activities started at your own institution, it is helpful to answer the following:

- What are the best ways for your campus to use professional teams to develop?

- How can you change the reward system to encourage faculty members to share their workload—and how can you fairly compensate them for their work on this new enterprise?

Summing Up

There is no doubt that the demands on faculty members are changing. This is happening despite faculty's intentions or institutional leaders' intentions. Many faculty members are creating, sharing, and importing electronic materials to ensure that their students have the best learning tools possible. With ubiquitous access to the Internet, faculty and students are experimenting and seeking more efficient ways to work together. Automated course management tools are commonplace, while electronically mediated tutoring and grading services are becoming more popular (see Chapter 8). Students are sharing files with one another. This can be good for everyone, if faculty members can free up more of their time to work directly with the students who need the most assistance. But institutional policies must keep up with modern-day practices.

In a time of rapid change, there is never a perfect solution to the mismatch between policy and practice. Still, vigilance on the part of academic leaders can help mitigate adverse effects. Regularly scheduled policy audits may be time-consuming, but as with most things that affect the way we work, they can save time in the long run. Defining a new vision for the faculty on your campus could help engage your teaching community and uncover the policy barriers that are currently impeding student service innovations.

Endnote

1) My thanks to Sharmila Basu Conger (policy analyst, State Higher Education Executive Officers Organization) for writing the original report of the project, from which I drew heavily.

References

Daniel, J. S. (1996). *Mega-universities and knowledge media: Technology strategies for higher education.* London, England: Kogan Page.

EduTools. (2006a). *Policy details: Arkansas Tech University.* Retrieved July 13, 2006, from: www.edutools.info/compare.jsp?pj=6&i=145

EduTools. (2006b). *Policy details: University of Wisconsin System.* Retrieved July 13, 2006, from: www.edutools.info/compare.jsp?pj=6&i=142

Harper, G. K. (2001). *The copyright crash course.* Retrieved July 13, 2006, from: www.utsystem.edu/ogc/Intellectualproperty/cprtindx.htm

Green, K. C. (2005). *The 2005 national survey of information technology in U.S. higher education.* Encino, CA: The Campus Computing Project.

Jaschik, S. (2006, March 6). Moving to 'conversion.' *Inside Higher Ed.* Retrieved July 13, 2006, from: http://insidehighered.com/news/2006/03/06/aftnea

Lovett, M. (2006). Manuscript submitted for publication.

Muffo, J. A., & Taylor, C. D. (1999). *Report on the Mathematics Emporium at Virginia Tech.* Blacksburg, VA: Virginia Polytechnic Institute and State University, Office of the Provost and Vice President for Academic Affairs.

Silverstein, S. (2006, January 17). The iPod took my seat. *Los Angeles Times*, p. A1.

Southern Regional Education Board. (2005, December). *SREB fact book bulletin: Reporting significant trends affecting education progress in the SREB states.* Atlanta, GA: Author

Twigg, C. A. (2003, July/August). Improving quality and reducing cost: Designs for effective learning. *Change, 35*(4), 22–29.

Young, J. R. (2006, January 25). Apple releases free software for distributing class materials. *The Chronicle of Higher Education, 52*(22), A36.

5 ··· Accountability and Assuring Quality

Sally M. Johnstone

Some stakeholders believe that transparency of performance is the most significant issue facing American higher education.

——*David Longanecker, WICHE*

The general public seems to be losing faith in higher education's ability to produce well-educated graduates at a reasonable cost. The Association of Governing Boards of Universities and Colleges (see www.agb.org) listed "accountability to the public" as one of its top 10 public policy issues for 2005–2006. Legislators in several states are asking for evidence that public colleges and universities are using their money wisely. Recently, there have been several highly visible scandals concerning salaries for top officials whose jobs do not make sense to those outside the higher education community. People want to know they are getting a good deal from their investments in colleges and universities.

In the mid 1990s Governors Mike Leavitt (Utah) and Roy Romer (Colorado) and their colleagues in the Western Governors' Association became so concerned about accountability in higher education that they decided to tackle the problem head on. The conversations at that time revolved around several issues. Part of the concept of accountability is directly related to how well an organization serves its public, yet the overwhelming perception at the time was that public higher education institutions were not being responsive to the needs of the citizenry of the states that supported them. The institutions seemed unable to change. The governors were told by their states' institutions that part of the reason for their inability to do things differently lay with their accreditors. So the governors began asking: Who are these accreditors? Who gives them this authority?

The western governors also noted the absence of any measurement of what students really learned during their academic careers (with the exception of students whose fields had licensing requirements). There did not seem to be any real evidence to support a cost-benefit analysis of the states' investments in higher education.

The governors decided to create an institution to address this lack of accountability. The Western Governors University (WGU; see www.wgu.edu) was designed to grant degrees and certifications that reflect workforce needs in the western states and are based on learning outcomes.

This new institution faced many challenges, but foremost among them was the problem of validating its certifications. In short, WGU needed accreditation. Because it was a multistate institution, serving 15 states (with offices in two of them), it did not fit neatly into any single regional accrediting association's territory. To sort things out, Governors Leavitt and Romer held a summit with the heads of the western accrediting associations—including the North Central Association, the Western Association of Schools and Colleges, and the Northwest Commission on Colleges and Universities—challenging them to be responsive to new methods of providing a high-quality education. In the end, these independent regional associations found a way to work together to evaluate—and eventually accredit—WGU.

I tell this story for two reasons. The first is to illustrate the frustration our elected officials sometimes feel with institutions of higher learning. The second is to show how the gatekeepers of quality for American colleges and universities are able to adapt. In the late 1990s, as a result of this experience and others—namely the growing use of information and communication technologies (ICTs) to connect students with institutions, regardless of their geographic locations—the regional accrediting community formed the Council of Regional Accrediting Commissions (C-RAC). C-RAC brings together the executive staff and chairs of each commission on a regular basis to sort out issues that affect all of them. For an entire century, these regional associations had worked indepen-

dently. As an indication of their adaptive trends, they collectively accepted the same set of *Principles of Good Practice for Electronically Delivered
Degree and Certificate Programs,* which had been authored for them by
WCET (2005). Each association might use the principles differently,
but they use them.

Institutional Quality Assurance and Accrediting

The regional accrediting organizations are still adapting and trying to
keep up with the institutional changes they are seeing. The following
essay shows how things have changed.

New Institutional Expectations Related to the Integration
of Technology
Steven Crow

In 2001–2002 the Higher Learning Commission engaged in a major
review and revision of its accreditation standards. Titled
"Restructuring Expectations: Accreditation, 2004," the project
engaged more than 1,000 people in a variety of conversations. An
invited "architecture task force" proposed the large outlines of the new
standards. Shortly after, six study teams collaborated through electronic bulletin boards to create broad policy papers on specific topics.
One team developed a paper to inform the commission about the
new standards and explain how they might account for (and be
responsive to) the impact of technology in learning and teaching.
About midway through the project, the chairs of the study teams
made presentations to the Board of Trustees commission staff and
with them studied the emerging draft of the proposed standards to see
how it could best incorporate the recommendations of the teams.

The other study team topics, which were mission, governance,
finances, diversity, and planning, would undoubtedly strike most in

the higher education community as being central to accreditation activities, while the impact of technology might seem relevant but somewhat tangential. At that time, despite the clear impact of computerization on higher education, accrediting agencies tended to view computerization as strongly related to administrative tasks, shifting the understanding of learning center/library contents and services, and somehow related to basic skills that college graduates should possess (i.e., the computer literacy needed for the workplace).

Without the recommendations of the study team, it is possible that the driving paradigm of the new standards could have focused on preparing students to live productively in a society increasingly shaped by new technologies. In other words, the new standards could have emerged from the belief that students need to be computer literate as a sort of general education skill, like effective writing and critical thinking, but that their educational experience need not be significantly shaped by technology.

The commission had already extended accreditation to a virtual institution and had within its membership a growing number of noncampus-based institutions. It was clear that if the new standards were to incorporate these institutions and others like them (and the Board of Trustees had made explicit its expectation that the new standards would include a broad universe of organizations offering higher learning), they needed to account for the potential of technology and its possible impact on the teaching and learning environments provided for students.

As the executive director of the commission, my hope for this study team was that it would wrestle with the accreditation associations' long history of linking accreditation to faculty status (full-time and part-time) and faculty roles (bundled and unbundled). The commission had been working with a set of general institutional requirements that dictated that a core of full-time, appropriately credentialed faculty was fundamental to any relationship with the agency. The accreditation of a virtual institution had stretched the commission's interpretation of the requirements almost to the breaking point. Ever hopeful, I decided to create a study team that would include participants committed to the value of a classroom education led by well-prepared faculty. The study team's report acknowledged that technology could shift traditional student-faculty relationships, but it did not propose a radical revisioning of faculty.

Instead, the study team asserted that technology would change the way faculty members teach and students engage in learning.

> Perhaps the primary overriding message of this report, especially as it relates to faculty roles in the future, is that the use of technology in teaching and learning is becoming independent of a student's location, and that all faculty—full-time and part-time, on campus or off campus, or a mixture—will need to be skilled in utilizing a number of new and emerging electronic technologies. (North Central Association Commission on Higher Learning, 2002, p. 3)

In short, the study team counseled the commission against making an easy connection between the new technologies and distance education. It asked us, instead, to consider the dramatic impact technology was having—and would continue to have—on every campus's learning environment. The report stepped back from proposing that every teaching faculty should become technologically competent, and carefully circumscribed some of its points by highlighting the dramatic differences among various institutions' missions and educational environments.

As the study team carefully and skillfully balanced excellent traditionally delivered education with the possibilities of enhanced learning through technology, it concluded that "at a minimum, it should be an expectation of an accredited institution in the 21st century that its faculty members be informed about and actively encouraged and supported in making appropriate uses of technology in creating effective learning environments" (North Central Association Commission on Higher Learning, 2002, p. 5).

Steven Crow is the executive director of the Higher Learning Commission of the North Central Association and serves on international teams to establish quality assurance agencies around the world.

....

This essay reflects many of the trends and activities discussed in Chapter 4. It is heartening to realize that the trends that many of us have watched for years are being incorporated into an institutional accountability system that is so widely used by traditional colleges and universities. The Higher Learning Commission (like other regional accrediting associations) is looking at the bigger picture with regard to how ICTs are changing the way the campus community works. The commission is not only reflecting current activities, but is trying to bring less advanced institutions up to speed.

Managing Accountability

Chapter 2 covers a number of issues around assessing the costs of various technologies. In this section I address the issue of how we manage the demands of different constituencies for accountability. When we talk to members of campus communities, we hear real concern about the pervasive use and costs of ICTs. The usual question is, "Why is the college spending money on software upgrades and new computers when that money could be used for fixing buildings, faculty salaries, better classrooms, more volumes in the library, more parking garages, or _____ (fill in the blank)?" These are real concerns, but if we do not find ways to keep our institutions up to speed with the rest of the connected world, it is unlikely we will continue to need all those parking garages.

When I raised these issues with my colleague, George Connick, he shared some interesting lessons learned from his pioneering work integrating ICTs into the campus over which he presided in the late 1980s and early 1990s.

....

Making the Difficult Choice to Integrate New Technology
George Connick

I would call this the fundamental challenge for all presidents—the classic bread or bullets policy decision. This is a choice between two "good things," both of which will benefit the institution in the short and long run.

As president, it helped me to put all issues and decisions (especially of this type) into a context that made sense for me. Once I understood the context, it was much easier to explain the decision. It didn't mean everyone agreed with the decision, but at least everyone knew my reason for it.

I always tried not to get caught in an either/or situation. I believed my job as president was roughly divided into two sections: 1) broad leadership responsibility that required thinking about how to nurture and develop the institution over time (with a focus on both physical and human infrastructure), and 2) the daily grind of meetings and decisions.

Investing in infrastructure is a long-term decision, while salaries are an annual, short-term issue.

I became president in 1985, just as the computer and technological revolution was launched. By and large, educators didn't see it coming—and when educational technology began to be seriously discussed, they appeared to be very frightened of it. I was routinely confronted by this technology-versus-people quandary.

I chose to invest in network technology in the short term, because it could build a critical part of the physical infrastructure for the long term. It was desired by students, faculty, and staff. It had a quick payoff and drove fundamental change and improvements for the institution.

As I advocated this method, I also developed a plan to address faculty salaries over a reasonable period of time (one to three years). I would point out to faculty the numerous ways in which they would benefit (including monetarily) from technology. No matter how logical the reason, there is very little you can say to make faculty feel better about not getting a salary increase. You have to make a choice—even if it means making the faculty think they come in second.

George Connick is president emeritus of the Education Network of Maine, the statewide distance learning network of the University of Maine System. He served as president of the University of Maine–Augusta from 1985–1994.

In an environment as complex as that of higher education, it is never easy to appease one's constituents, but when the investments are balanced among various groups, it is easier for everyone to understand. As George points out, it is vital to define the benefits of any new system for all members of the campus community that will be affected. Of course, this task becomes more challenging when you address constituents outside the institution. This is the problem faced by public institutions that are accountable to legislators. In the following essay, Patricia Cuocco and Steve Daigle of California State University describe a strategy for managing the expectations of legislators and the general public when making large investments in ICTs.

Accountability for Technology Investments to Policymakers
Patricia Cuocco and Steve Daigle

The Integrated Technology Strategy (ITS) is the framework within which California State University (CSU) has managed the investment of information technology goods and services for more than a

decade. Approved by the CSU Board of Trustees in March 1996,
the ITS supports an integrated electronic environment that enables
all CSU students, faculty, and staff to communicate with one another and interact with information resources from any place to any
place at any time.

CSU is still working with and building on the ITS framework
a decade later—an extraordinary achievement in the annals of higher education. The success of this framework can be attributed to a
number of factors. First and foremost is the fact that the ITS is just
that: a framework, not a plan. The former implies a living, evolving
structure; the latter, a static and stagnant document with a limited
shelf life.

Two other elements of the plan have contributed to its continued success—presidential leadership and the involvement of the
constituency.

Background

California State University (CSU) is the largest four-year institution
of higher education in the country, with 23 separate universities that
serve more than 405,000 students and employ more than 44,000
faculty and staff. The 1960 California Master Plan for Education
puts CSU in the middle tier of the state's public higher education
system, with the University of California and 109 community colleges the first and third tiers, respectively.

In the early 1990s, some of the forces that shaped higher education had a direct impact on CSU's decision to embrace information technology. First and foremost, a "tidal wave" of new students
was soon expected to seek admission. Estimates at the time indicated that enrollment could grow to more than 500,000 students by
2010. These students, many of them historically underserved (and
nontraditional), would demand more access to distributed forms of
learning and electronic information resources.

Second, the transition from Industrial Age to Information Age was almost complete, with the implications for higher education paralleling those for industry (i.e., a need for emphasis on productivity and client relationships). Third, because of state budgetary constraints and a decline in revenues for education, there was an increased emphasis on accountability for public funds. Finally, the exponential growth in and convergence of information and communication technologies were beginning to have an impact on society and culture (California State University, 1997).

ITS: Top-Down Leadership

In January 1993, then-chancellor Barry Munitz, reporting to the Board of Trustees, challenged CSU to "do things differently." It was an acknowledgement of societal change and the need to do more with less, and—perhaps more significantly—a call to move away from a culture of isolated campuses to one that capitalized on the size and strength of the system.

That same year, CSU campus presidents made some unprecedented decisions. They agreed that information technology was a strategic tool that could be leveraged in support of larger CSU goals and objectives. They also acknowledged that only a system-wide approach would maximize this leverage, and that the leadership for such an approach would have to come from them—not their subordinates, and not the Office of the Chancellor (the system-wide headquarters).

The presidents further decided that the notion of "have and have-not" campuses was unacceptable. In order to offer the best learning/teaching/scholarly and administrative environment for all CSU students, faculty, and staff, there had to be a baseline technological infrastructure in place at every campus.

ITS: Process

The ITS planning process was unique, but it can be replicated by a system or consortia of institutions committed to leveraging size and creating efficiencies. Several overarching premises have shaped the ITS since its inception. The ITS is not a plan per se, since there is no formal document or blueprint. Rather, the ITS is a framework within which a dynamic series of initiatives can be developed and implemented, and a systematic process for identifying priorities and evaluating progress.

Within this stable structure, the ITS adheres to a systematic planning process governed by five key elements: assumptions and principles, stakeholder collaboration, initiative filtering and prioritization, research and evaluation, and sustained leadership. This process was used to develop the initial list of initiative priorities, then replicated (with few exceptions) to produce a second wave of ITS initiatives in academic technology.

Assumptions and Principles

ITS began with a set of planning assumptions and principles. *Assumptions* are defined as "forces that will affect both the planning and implementation of information technology initiatives. Essentially, they represent the state of our operating environment whether we like it or not and regardless of what we do" (SCU, 1997, p. 16). Assumptions reflect stakeholders' pragmatic judgments about the external forces that impact the future direction of CSU. Accordingly, they are facts about the future, largely predictable conditions that will occur apart from any attempts to control them. Demographic trends are a good example. The assumptions fall into six major categories: academic, political, social, economic, organizational, and technical.

Principles provide the criteria used to create, select, design, and implement ITS initiatives and projects. Unlike assumptions, principles are matters of choice and values. There are three types of planning principles: overarching (strategic), priority (tactical), and design (operational). An example of each type follows:

- *Overarching.* Faculty, students, and staff should have easy, well-supported electronic access to the data and information necessary to perform their university functions, regardless of CSU location.

- *Priority.* Preference should be given to initiatives that facilitate partnering among campuses for the design, implementation, and use of common applications.

- *Design.* Data should be collected once, electronically, as close to their points of origin as possible.

Stakeholder Collaboration

As noted, the ITS could not have been created without presidential leadership, nor could it have been institutionalized without significant constituency involvement. In the collegial environment of higher education, institutions that wish to emulate this model would be wise to take this lesson to heart.

Initiative/Project Filtering

The heart of the planning process involved identifying a series of priority initiatives or projects that would achieve the overall goals of CSU and move the system as a whole toward a particular type of information technology environment.

Research and Evaluation

The development of the ITS, and the desire to see its benefits disseminated to the widest possible group of stakeholders, fostered a culture of evidence within IT management at CSU. Measurement, assessment, and accountability are the ultimate tests of the ITS.

Its Vision and Framework

As previously mentioned, the initial idea behind ITS was to produce an integrated electronic environment that enabled all CSU students, faculty, and staff to communicate with one another and to interact with information resources from any place, to any place, at any time.

Higher education institutions have traditionally had four resources: academic programs, faculty and staff personnel, physical facilities, and fiscal budgets. But in the modern world, technology has become the fifth critical resource that institutions need to attain their mission. In essence, the ITS was based on the assumption that information technology is that fifth strategic, institutional resource. As a result, it had to be planned and implemented in a comprehensive, integrated fashion.

The following outcomes were targeted through the ITS (CSU, 1997, p. 9):

- *Excellence in Learning and Teaching.* Infusing technology into the learning and teaching processes to make them more effective, increasing faculty and institutional collaboration and resource sharing, and enhancing student and faculty access to information resources and to each other.

- *Quality of the Student Experience.* Using technology to enhance the overall experience of students, from recruitment to graduation from CSU.

- *Administrative Productivity and Quality.* Reengineering and redesigning administrative support and the delivery of information technology to achieve greater effectiveness at a lower cost.

- *Personal Productivity.* Providing technology tools and capabilities to increase and enhance the effectiveness and efficiency of students, faculty, and staff as they perform their university functions.

Over the years, the ITS has been portrayed as a pyramid, with the four outcomes at the apex, the prerequisite infrastructure at the base, and a series of enabling initiatives in the middle (Figure 5.1). The outcomes, tightly linked to the CSU mission, never change. The components within the infrastructure are also very stable (its physical wiring and electronics, workstation hardware and software, campus networks, student, faculty, and staff training, and technical support), although new components are introduced as old initiatives are absorbed and emerging requirements (e.g., security and identity management) necessitate additional efforts. The academic, administrative, and infrastructure initiatives represent the dynamic nature of the ITS framework. New initiatives begin as need dictates, and previous initiatives become a permanent part of the infrastructure and its operations once they are completed.

Figure 5.1 shows the original first-wave initiatives of the ITS and the second-wave initiatives adopted in 2004. The bottom layer of the pyramid depicts progress in meeting minimum baseline standards in each of the elements of the IT infrastructure as of June 30, 2005.

ITS Initiatives: Progress to Date
Technology Infrastructure

Not long into the planning process, it became evident that the academic and administrative outcomes of the ITS could not be achieved without the necessary technology infrastructure. In that sense, it is a prerequisite, first on the critical path toward achieving the four outcomes. Yet the infrastructure also carries independent benefits for students, faculty, and staff in the form of personal productivity tools. It has seven major components, each of which contains metrics that define what stakeholders determine to be the acceptable, or minimum, baseline capability:

- *Physical infrastructure*—the pathways, wiring, and associated electronics that are the foundation for a connected campus

Figure 5.1.
The Integrated Technology Strategy

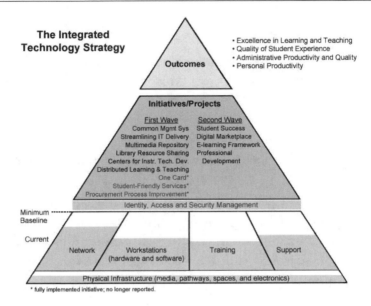

* fully implemented initiative; no longer reported.

- *Network access*—a voice, data, and video network (intracampus and intercampus) that connects schools with each other and the rest of the world and forms connections between buildings, floors, and workstations at each CSU location

- *Hardware and equipment access*—the digital hardware and related equipment required to provide each individual with appropriate access to electronic information resources

- *Software and applications access*—the core software tools and disciplinary applications that are critical to the teaching and learning process

- *User training*—ongoing programs that provide continuous skill building in the use of information technology for everyone in CSU

- *Support services*—ubiquitous access to 24/7 support services that allow students, faculty, and staff to ask questions and solve hardware, software, and network problems

- *Middleware*—the security and access management controls that link hardware, software, and data repositories (This is an emerging and critical area of concern, one that was not apparent when the original ITS was developed.)

Network development is one of the great CSU success stories. It began in the 1980s with an intercampus network known as CSUNet. In the 1990s, it was expanded to include the state's community colleges and hundreds of K–12 schools and administrative offices. These days, CSU helps lead the California Research and Education Network (CalREN), a high-performance network that links virtually all K–12 schools and most of the major public and private institutions of higher education in the state.

Administrative Systems

As implementation progressed, the need for an administrative infrastructure became obvious. The Common Management System initiative (CMS) is the largest administrative Enterprise Resource Planning (ERP) project of its kind in American higher education. Prior to the CMS implementation, CSU campuses had outdated financial systems, inefficient, manually operated personnel systems, and student administration systems that were different for each campus. Campuses maintained their own data centers for managing these administrative systems. The CMS introduced standardized software, common data elements, and best practices for human resources, financial, and student systems, while also allowing limited variations to suit each campus's needs. In addition, the CMS initiative created a single consolidated, outsourced data center in an innovative and cost-effective manner. This data center was the first of its kind in higher education.

The primary objectives of this software and database standardization and data center centralization were to improve the quality and efficiency of administrative services. Improved administrative services support improved academic processes. For one thing, they assist faculty advisors by providing comprehensive, up-to-date information about students' academic progress, which helps them give students better guidance. They also make it easier for faculty to maintain online profiles, aiding in their retention, tenure, and promotion. The student administration module enables students to monitor their admission status, register for classes, check their grades, and perform audits to chart their progress toward a degree (or to make corrections in their courses to facilitate a timely graduation).

As of 2006, 21 campuses have implemented the human resources and financial modules, while 10 have implemented the student software.

Academic Technology

Initiatives in this category are student centered and directly address two of the ITS goals: excellence in teaching and learning and the quality of the student experience outside the classroom. They include:

- *Collaborative learning and teaching*—defines, selects, and implements common tools to support CSU faculty and students in an anytime, anywhere environment. This includes email systems, conferencing capabilities, document transfer of electronic class materials, and other learning technologies.

- *Centers for faculty technology training*—establishes faculty development centers that focus on helping faculty use technology in the instructional process.

- *The MERLOT multimedia repository*—creates a repository of digital instructional materials that CSU develops, purchases, or borrows to support learning and teaching needs. The MERLOT repository is a central clearinghouse used by CSU faculty and students (as well as faculty and students from other educational systems around the world) to access instructional materials.

- *Library unified information access system*—provides a single library user interface for CSU faculty and students. It uses industry standards to provide consistent access to a wide variety of library materials and catalogs, both inside and outside CSU.

- *Information competency*—promotes the ability to use digital technology, communication tools, and/or networks. This includes the ability to define, access, evaluate, integrate, manage, create, and communicate information ethically and responsibly. During 2003 and 2004, CSU took the lead in forming a partnership with the Educational Testing Service (ETS) and several other colleges and universities to develop a web-based tool that assessed information and communication technology (ICT) literacy.

- *Student-friendly services*—uses information technology to facilitate interactions with the university (in area such as communication, admission, registration, and scheduling) for students, potential students, and their parents and counselors. The initial project used a single electronic student admissions application form, known as CSUMentor, that connected to all CSU campuses. CSUMentor simplified the admission process and improved CSU's response time.

- *One Card*—provides CSU faculty, students, and staff on some campuses with a single plastic card that can be used for facility and service access (e.g., meals, security, etc.), long distance telephone calls, and debit card purchases.

Accountability

The cost of providing a physical infrastructure of the kind detailed here was (and is) considerable. CSU investigated public and private partnerships, but this did not prove viable for a variety of reasons, many of them having to do with the culture of academia. Fortunately, the economic situation in California improved, and voters passed a general obligation bond for capital spending. Here, again, presidential leadership played a deciding role. The CSU presidents determined that the highest priority for bond capital spending would be the installation of a minimum baseline infrastructure at every CSU campus.

Legislatures understand buildings—bricks and mortar—quite well, and they understand the justifications for building them. This is not necessarily true with conduits, cables, and connecting electronics. The California state legislature rightly demanded that CSU show, over time, how an investment in its physical infrastructure would benefit students, faculty, and staff.

The existence of the ITS framework facilitated the accountability process. Through iterative discussion, the legislature agreed that CSU would measure the progress of the various ITS initiatives, the benefits of which could not be spread throughout the system without a robust infrastructure.

In 1999 CSU agreed to conduct annual reviews of the ITS and make formal reports, called "Measures of Success" (MOS), to the California legislature. An extensive series of metrics was developed, and baseline data were collected in 2000. Annual ITS progress is now measured against that baseline. System-wide databases and annual campus surveys inform the MOS reports, providing a broad and detailed picture of the technology resources and services available across the system. (The MOS reports can be viewed online: http://its.calstate.edu/documents/Data_Collection/I_Reports_MO S/Measure_of_Success.shtml) In just a short time, the MOS reports have emerged as among the most visible and comprehensive examples of public accountability in institutions of higher education.

Other assessment activities include participation in various national surveys on information technology that compare CSU to other institutions, and biennial user surveys conducted among representative samples of CSU students, faculty, and staff. These surveys measure the use of technology, attitudes toward technology, and satisfaction with various aspects of technology available on campus or through system resources such as CalREN, the statewide education network.

While accountability is never inexpensive, being able to prove that your activities are worthwhile—especially to those charged with dispensing taxpayer dollars—is invaluable.

Patricia Cuocco is senior director for technology policy, planning, and advice, and Steve Daigle is senior research associate in the Division of Information Technology Services, both at the CSU Office of the Chancellor.

Demonstrating accountability is not a simple task. As Patricia and Steve make clear in the CSU example, it takes extensive planning and the fortitude to stick to that plan. Few institutional leaders have to operate on the same scale as CSU, but I think theirs is a good model that can be applied to many different situations. Central to this model is the framing of accountability measures. CSU started by identifying the critical issues for their target group (legislators) and set up ways to measure those things. From that point on, everything else flowed

Student Accountability

Many aspects of accountability involve students and what they actually do. The advent of ICT has changed a lot about the way we look at and measure a student's performance, ultimately calling into question the integrity of an institution's degree. The use of ICTs for aspects of class-level instruction may be increasing the tendency for students to take courses from multiple institutions as they work toward achieving their academic goals. Cliff Adelman of the U.S. Department of Education has been tracking cohort groups of students for more than a decade to sort out what they actually do in continuing their education beyond high school. In his latest update of this work, he notes:

> Postsecondary attendance patterns among traditional-age students have become far more complex, with near-ly 60% of undergraduates attending more than one institution, and 35% of them crossing states in the process; community college transfer rates have risen nearly 10 percentage points; one of eight undergraduates based in four-year institutions using community colleges to fill in pieces of their curriculum, and another eight percent "swirling" back and forth between the four-year and two-year sectors. Dual-enrollment while in high school, credit-by-examination, and the use of summer terms all added to the dynamic mix of time and space that marked student pathways in the 1990s. (Adelman, 2006, pp. xv–xvi)

Students seem to be taking more and more online courses, frequently using resources from multiple institutions. Traditional on-campus students are filling out their required courses with online classes that fit their schedules and preferences. These online classes may or may not come from the institution at which a student expects to earn a degree. Students expect online courses to count toward the degree they plan to earn. The complex—and sometimes costly—process of transferring credits between institutions is probably not part of any student's initial thinking when he or she decides to sign up for online classes:

> The college degree . . . is coming to represent a differ-
> ent type of experience: the completion of an idiosyn-
> cratic amalgam of educational experiences selected by
> the student from a number of unrelated institutions
> and delivered by a mix of technological as well as phys-
> ical means. (Eaton, 2002, p. 6)

What does this mean for the quality of students' learning experience, and how does it affect the granting of degrees from specific institutions? Some colleagues and I tried to examine this question a few years ago. Peter Ewell, Karen Paulson, and I noted that the solution may lie in awarding degrees that are not based on the number of credit hours a student earned, but rather on the competencies that he or she demonstrated (Johnstone, Ewell, & Paulson, 2002). The impediments to this possible solution are not insubstantial, but we do have examples of relatively successful applications of outcome assessments having real currency in higher education. Advanced Placement test scores, for example, are portable and recognized by most institutions. An early example of this type of exam was seen at the University of Chicago in the 1930s (Johnstone et al.). At that time, students could test out of large portions of the curriculum based on comprehensive examinations developed and administered by the university's examiner's office.

In the 1960s several institutions were founded and accredited based entirely on examination-based achievement, including Excelsior (formerly Regents) University in New York, Thomas Edison State College in New Jersey, and Charter Oak State College in Connecticut. All of these institutions confer traditional academic degrees, with grades that reflect course equivalencies. But the standard that backs those grades is based directly on student performance, using criterion-referenced examinations.

In Chapter 7 we talk more about new students and their expectations. Our best guess is that these students will not amass credentials (or learning experiences) at just one institution. As a result, institutions that grant credentials must develop ways to ensure that students have mastered a coherent body of knowledge. That is harder to do when students are bundling courses from multiple institutions. The most straightforward way to address this is to change academic accounting from a seat-time-based approach to a competency-based approach. With the latter approach, each student would be required to demonstrate his or her subject-specific knowledge and ability in areas that require oral and written literacy. The underlying change may seem radical, but in many ways, it is just another evolution. In many cases, faculty members already specify learning objectives for their courses. More specific course objectives may evolve into course competencies, and eventually into program-level and degree-level competencies that are credible to employers and other institutions. In this way, a new approach to academic currency—one based on actual student learning—can be forged. As our colleague, Russell Edgerton,[1] reminds us:

> The key features of our approach to quality assurance are the end product of a long history of evolution. The pattern has been for a practice to emerge at one historical moment and then become accepted as "the way things are" locked into the system by the expectations of multiple constituencies both inside and outside academic institutions. (Johnstone et al., 2002, p. 27)

Other learning industries have bridged this apparent chasm. Cisco Systems, for example, has an educational component (as do other high-tech companies that need to keep people up to date on new technologies). Although Cisco staff members do not teach classes, they create instructional materials in multiple formats. Private vendors then offer classes (either face to face or online) to students, using materials produced by Cisco Systems. Students may also choose to learn this material without formal classes. When a student is prepared, he or she may sit for an examination given by an organization that does not offer the classes, but uses Cisco's assessments. If the testing organization ensures the student's competency, Cisco Systems grants the student a credential—one that has real value in the workplace. In fact, many colleges and universities have partnered with Cisco to incorporate Cisco's materials into university-level engineering programs, giving their graduates additional advantages.[2]

It is interesting to note that when Congress passed the Budget Reconciliation Act at the end of 2005, it included language that allowed the federal government to recognize as postsecondary institutions those that award degrees without actually teaching classes. This means that institutions that award degrees based on an accumulation of credit from other institutions or through the assessment of competencies are eligible for competitive federal grants, and their students are eligible for federal financial aid.

This change could give rise to an entirely new set of private companies that offer degrees. However, for their degrees to be valid they will have to ensure the quality of their procedures. They will also have to be accountable to the same public pressures that are experienced by our current higher education institutions. Whatever happens, this does suggest that we have begun to look at things in a new way.

Summing Up

While higher education has long been concerned with ensuring quality and accountability, things seem to be moving particularly rapidly at present. Since the rest of world is also moving quickly, this is not a surprise. There are shifts taking place in higher education that will require some real creativity and adaptability. What's happening at our regional accrediting associations demonstrates the changes wrought by the use of ICTs on campuses and throughout the world. As students (and their legislative representatives) begin to rely on multiple sources for their education, they will still expect to receive degrees—no matter where they took the course. This poses a problem for colleges and universities that want to protect the quality of their credentials. The solution may lie in shifting away from courses and credit hours and toward learning assessments.

One thing is certain: Higher education is faced with another intriguing challenge that will keep us all creatively engaged for years to come.

Endnotes

1) Russell Edgerton is a honored observer of higher education trends. Among other roles in academe, he served as the president of the American Association for Higher Education from 1977–1997.

2) Sharmila Basu Conger worked with me on a project a few years ago that enabled us to track how high tech industries managed their credentialing. Sharmila is now a policy analyst at the State Higher Education Executive Officers organization, but worked at WCET when this research was done.

References

Adelman, C. (2006). *The toolbox revisited: Paths to degree completion from high school through college.* Washington, DC: U.S. Department of Education.

California State University. (1997). *Integrated technology strategy: Planning and implementation.* Retrieved July 14, 2006, from: http://its.calstate.edu/systemwide_it_resources/its_report.pdf

Eaton, J. S. (2002). *Maintaining the delicate balance: Distance learning, higher education accreditation, and the politics of self-regulation.* Washington, DC: American Council on Education.

Johnstone, S. M., Ewell, P., & Paulson, K. (2002). *Student learning as academic currency.* Washington, DC: American Council on Education.

North Central Association Commission on Higher Learning. (2002). *NCA study team report: The impact of technology in learning and teaching.* Chicago, IL: The Higher Learning Commission.

Western Cooperative for Educational Telecommunications. (2005). *Principles of good practice for electronically offered academic degree and certificate programs.* Retrieved July 14, 2006, from: http://www.wcet.info /projects/balancing/principles.asp

6 ··· Joining Others: Lessons for Consortial Relationships

Sally M. Johnstone

Academe is known for saying, "publish or perish." I say, "partner or perish."

—Mary Sue Coleman, president of the University of Michigan
(Capriccioso, 2006)

Most institutions of higher education are used to competing with each other. No matter where they rank in popular magazine ratings, public institutions have to compete for state funding, research universities have to compete for federal grants, and all institutions have to compete for students. Most campus leaders are used to thinking of other institutions in terms of competition instead of cooperation. Yet with the current need for accountability and efficiency, we must start thinking about which activities we can share.

When institutions decide to work together, there are a number of ways that are enabled by information and communication technologies (ICTs). Some of the ways institutions can work together include:

- Saving money with the collective purchase and licensing of hardware, software, and technical services

- Allowing faculty to work with their peers on site and at other institutions to create course materials

- Allowing institutions and schools to share courses

- Allowing the development of electronic services for students and faculty

- Creating resources in open formats that aid in institutional recognition and mission fulfillment

While it is easy to make a list and dream up new ways campuses can work together, it is another thing to actually make these things happen. I have asked people who have developed and run various types of consortia to share their collective accomplishments with you, and I hope you find their stories interesting and insightful. Their consortia range from formally developed and funded statewide higher education networks to less formal collections of shared materials. One consortium started as a typical statewide electronic network that evolved to facilitate intercampus collaborations. Another began as a statewide service and purchasing organization and has become a major resource for campuses in that state. A larger, multistate consortium links students at various campuses, enabling them to take courses their home campuses do not offer. And an even broader consortium helps link faculty worldwide, allowing them to share electronic information for use in face-to-face or distributed learning courses. One consortium to which I want to bring your attention is a much looser confederation of universities, colleges, and departments that is making its academic materials available for the world to see and use.

Some of the earliest statewide consortia were developed to create electronic networks between campuses. As indicated in the following essay about Indiana's network, a useful consortium needs to have a real purpose behind it, and it must be accountable to its members. As college and university leaders whose institutions are members of consortia, you cannot be passive. You must engage your staff and other members of your consortia to ensure you are getting what you need. If you do not, it is unlikely the consortium will evolve as your needs change.

The Indiana Higher Education Telecommunications System
Susan B. Scott

It all began in 1961, with astronomy. Purdue University had no one to teach introductory astronomy, but Indiana University had an eminent astronomer who was also a gifted teacher. The two universities contracted with Indiana Bell to construct a video microwave link between Bloomington and West Lafayette so that students at Purdue University could become part of the "live" Indiana University classes.

That simple, successful experiment laid the groundwork for an institutional collaboration that has grown over four decades to encompass all of Indiana's colleges and universities and most forms of educational technology: the Indiana Higher Education Telecommunication System (IHETS).

In 1967 the Indiana General Assembly authorized the institutions (at their request) to create IHETS as a self-governed organization, with an expectation of multiple technologies to come. The assembly also allocated funds to the project, helping to provide a stable baseline of financial support. The first network IHETS created (in 1968) was an intercampus telephone system that has since helped the institutions save millions of dollars in long-distance charges. Its affordability also encouraged intercampus voice and data communication. It seemed only natural, then, that IHETS should add an audio conferencing function to the telephone network during the gas crunch of the late 1970s. The robust network continued to meet members' needs for data communication until the 1990 decision to establish a dedicated Internet Protocol (IP) network.

An intercampus video network launched in 1969 helped regional campuses handle the onslaught of baby boomers in the late 1960s and early 1970s. The network's existence sparked creative thinking about other applications. New audiences might be reached by extending the network from its campus end points. The network could provide continuing medical education for physicians in hospitals and clinics, graduate engineering classes for people in various industries and at government agencies, MBA and nursing classes for other hospital and industry employees, graduate education for teachers and school administrators, Advanced Placement classes for high school students, and real-time agricultural news and education to Cooperative Extension Service county offices throughout the state. These work sites needed to make only one technology investment to receive programs from all the universities.

Moreover, new classes could be developed by connecting faculty and administrators from different institutions. The results included a basic mass communications course, a specialized family and consumer law course for human services professionals, noncredit career education seminars for K–12 employees, and occupational health and safety administration training for college staffers. In a typical scenario, one institution might oversee the financial aspects of a course, another would be the primary producer, and several others would plan and deliver the content. Faculty members who collaborated with colleagues at other institutions and invested time in learning more about pedagogy and instructional design found that their on-campus teaching improved as well.

Throughout the 1970s and 1980s, IHETS's reach expanded, along with the use of its services. Put simply, its institutions' ability to attract more students encouraged the institutions to develop more courses and degree programs, which attracted additional learners. As a result, IHETS needed to find newer, more flexible technologies to sustain this growth. At the time, Instructional Television Fixed Service (ITFS) offered the most economical way to deliver instruction beyond the system's end points. But when rural locations became interested in the service, they often found they had to install expensive towers to receive the signals. A $20,000 investment was often too much for these small schools, despite high need. Programming expanded further, and it soon became clear that four channels weren't enough, so from 1992 to 1995, IHETS moved the whole network to satellite, which doubled capacity and dramatically reduced connection costs. When interest later shifted from one-way video/two-way audio to two-way video/audio, IHETS reduced the number of its channels again, saving enough money to add videoconferencing.

IHETS also began to implement an IP data network, which was recognized from the outset as being potentially important for instruction as well as for research and administration. In 1992 only higher education was interested in IP networking. By 1997, however, numerous K–12 schools, public libraries, and state agencies had seen the benefit of common transmission protocols and paths. The IHETS network ultimately became the nucleus of a dramatically expanded state network that served the entire public sector with converged voice, video, and data service.

In 1992 responding to criticism that they had focused too much on graduate programs (and not enough on undergraduate offerings), the institutions began to use the program-coordinating part of IHETS to expand educational opportunities across the state. Out of this endeavor grew an unprecedented service, the Indiana College Network (ICN), which was intended to help residents locate programs of interest and cross-register among institutions as seamlessly as possible. ICN featured an accessible interinstitutional database of courses and programs, a central service to handle inquiries and broker students and campuses, a network of local learning centers that offered support to students engaged in distance learning, and a human network of distance learning coordinators at all campuses.

As the focus on undergraduate offerings intensified, campuses began drawing on their partner institution's courses (especially those in general education) when they developed new associate's and bachelor's degree programs. In the span of a decade, the institutions amassed nearly 2,500 courses and more than 70 degree programs for distance learners, with classes equally distributed between the associate, baccalaureate, and master's degree levels. Another 73 certificate and endorsement programs were also available. In 1994 there were 4,300 distance enrollments; by 2004, there were 100,000—and their ranks are still growing.

The consortium helped facilitate the sharing of faculty development activities while its institutions were still building capacity. Once most campuses developed their own faculty support centers, IHETS concentrated on supporting the collaboration of the instructional technologists themselves. In the mid-1990s, IHETS focused on building baseline awareness and capacity among student services personnel; now it fills a convening role for problem resolution. For several years, IHETS administered a program of small grants to faculty for the development of new classes or modules; its members continue to share best practices and recognize outstanding accomplishments.

The catalyst in Indiana (as elsewhere) was the introduction of the Internet. With IHETS providing solid Internet connectivity and helping faculty members take advantage of new web-based tools, even smaller campuses began to break into the online learning arena, serving on- and off-campus students. The rapid shift to all things digital, however, has raised new questions about the role and value of IHETS to its members.

Throughout the development of IHETS, its services have tended to be those which no single institution could easily afford unless they joined forces. Now, IHETS's future may have more to do with applications than networks. For example, the interinstitutional video network that originally gave rise to IHETS is being replaced with a large-scale shared web-conferencing service dubbed IHETS Interactive—an application rather than a physical network.

The easy answer to "Why collaborate?" is nearly always, "To save money." Most pundits agree that the halcyon days of ready and sufficient funding for higher education are gone, and as long as vendors offer reduced unit costs for large sales, aggregating demand can result in lowered costs for all participants. In fact, one tier of the new IHETS Interactive service is expected to provide overflow for campuses' baseline services and handle joint licensing arrangements to reduce costs. IHETS may also host applications to help institutions manage their bandwidth use, as such services are bandwidth intensive.

With its widely diverse membership, IHETS is a microcosm of adoption patterns. Indiana University, Purdue University, and the University of Notre Dame tend to be on the cutting edge, developing new applications before other institutions even recognize a need, so they are more likely to collaborate with other research universities. The next generation varies by size (including medium-sized institutions such as Ball State University, Indiana State University, or Indiana University–Purdue University Fort Wayne) or by mission (engineering and technology strongholds such as the Rose-Hulman Institute of Technology and Purdue University–Calumet, liberal arts institutions such as DePauw University and Earlham College, or the statewide community college system like Ivy Tech). Even before mainstream adoption, it's usually possible to pull together a critical mass of institutions that want to collaborate despite superficial market competition. By the time smaller schools are ready to adopt such services, the shared service makes it easier for them to get up to speed. In the meantime, the original developers have moved on to their next project but may still have lingering niche users.

Through IHETS's network and applications services and its forum for discussion of needs and strategies, Indiana's colleges and universities have used IHETS to reduce costs, leverage expertise, and serve broader audiences. But as financial pressures constrain their ability to keep up with the technology-related costs of being in the mainstream (e.g., ERP systems, course management systems, e-portfolios, escalating web services, security, support for faculty and students, digital library resources, support for multiple platforms and applications in decentralized environments, the retention of competent network staff, etc.), institutions will need to reexamine their assumptions about related strategies, including outsourcing, group purchases, and sharing expertise.

Today IHETS is not the same organization it was in 1967, visionary though that was. The lessons its institutions have learned over the years either validate those early assumptions or suggest steps to take for the future. Here are some of the most important:

- Focusing on real (rather than hypothetical) needs helps institutional leaders justify their participation and avoid a "build-it-and-they-will-come" syndrome.

- All institutional members must respect each other's autonomy. No member institution is required to participate in any IHETS service. In fact, voluntary participation makes it easier to value individual differences and similarities and identify contributions from partners who might otherwise be overlooked. Taking the time to develop collaborative foundations in nonthreatening ways helps ensure long-term success.

- Focusing on the reasons for the collaboration instead of on the specifics of the service provided can allow unexpected opportunities to emerge. Over the years, emphasizing the purposes of the IHETS video network has made possible several shifts in technology, whereas retaining a narrow focus would have resulted in continuous, expensive improvements to outmoded or irrelevant technologies.

- Engaging institutional leadership (while respecting the demands on leaders' time) boosts accountability and helps ensure that assumptions are always being challenged. Collaboration is often easiest for marginal services; leaders' authority is needed to encourage efficiency around core services.

In 2005 IHETS engaged in critical self-study, beginning a new strategic visioning and planning process that would extend through 2006. Institutional leaders will need to stay engaged in the process—helping to govern it, or conducting periodic reality checks—if the emerging system is to continue fostering collaboration among colleges and universities. Higher education's need to manage its technology investments has become too critical to ignore or delegate away.

Susan B. Scott is the chief operating officer for the Indiana College Network at the Indiana Higher Education Telecommunication System.

As noted in Chapter 5, in the mid-1990s the governors of the western states formed a virtual university that brought 16 states together to provide higher education resources to underserved populations and create a different credentialing system (which the governors thought might be more effective for the states' workforce needs). Their activities ended up spawning consortia and virtual universities all over the country. One example, which took place in Connecticut, was not atypical. Again, a group of people in the higher education community realized they could accomplish more working together than they could by going it alone. Supported by a small grant from the Sloan Foundation, they convinced the state legislature to support the development of distance learning courses at their colleges and universities. The Connecticut General Assembly initially gave the consortium $200,000, half of which went directly into course grants, and the other half into running the general organization. Today, that consortium has 19 employees, receives an annual amount of $600,000 from the Connecticut General Assembly (plus another $340,000 in capital equipment dollars), and earns $1.3 million per year. The story of its evolution—told in the following essay by Ed Klonoski—sheds light on how institutions have changed in the past decade.

....

Connecticut Distance Learning Consortium
Ed Klonoski

As learners became more savvy and online programs began to emerge to meet their needs, the Connecticut Distance Learning Consortium (CTDLC), like the numerous other virtual universities that were created in the late 1990s, was designed to encourage collaboration among schools that used distance learning courses and programs (Epper & Garn, 2003). The founding assumptions of the CTDLC included collective policy generation, shared technology, statewide faculty training, avoidance of program duplication, and even the dispensation of state development dollars (Klonoski, 2001a). Our membership included two- and four-year public and private colleges, and our nine-year history afforded us a number of opportunities to collaborate with (and foster collaboration with) the Connecticut educational community and the higher education community as a whole. Our story provides some interesting insight into how institutional collaboration has evolved over the years. In revisiting it, we may even get a glimpse of what will happen in the future.

In Connecticut we began with three essential collaborative challenges. We needed to learn how to train faculty in distance learning practices and technologies, amass satisfaction data on our new online learners, and share our technology with one another. Fortunately, our early distance learning efforts tapped an unmet demand, so we could still retain dissatisfied students while improving our courses. My favorite response to our earliest assessment efforts was from the student who replied, "This online course is the worst course I ever took. I have signed up for two more next semester."

For those early distance learning students, convenience and flexibility outweighed quality. But faculty understood that, in the long run, this wasn't going to be enough. Everyone needed to learn and improve, so the faculty demanded training in course management technologies and best practices in online pedagogy. It was not hard to convince faculty and administrators that training was necessary, and since there were not too many people available who knew how to do it, the CTDLC was called on to train faculty at a number of Connecticut institutions. Collaborating in this manner really helped the campuses, as they did not have to create and finance their own training programs.

CTDLC also collected student satisfaction data and related information for all of the online courses offered in the state. We did this because it seemed valuable to our members, and because our participation in the U.S. Department of Education Demonstration Program in Financial Aid demanded it. In the end we provided our institutions with information they never could have obtained on their own. For example, we were able to tell them that their early adopters were predominantly female, and that they tended to use multiple institutions and delivery vehicles to accelerate their progress toward a degree. What's more, 25% percent of those students took online courses from multiple institutions in the same semester. Here we were, creating courses and watching enrollment grow at a rate of more than 70% a year, and our online students often had more experience than we did! These users ended up determining the quality of many of our initiatives, as they already came to the courses with certain expectations and experiences. We had little trouble convincing institutions that they would be better off if they collaborated to meet students' needs: They were already having a hard time keeping up.

It was equally simple to get the institutions to collaborate around delivery technology. At the time, schools were beginning to purchase course management systems, but even in the early days, they were tripping over costs, technical issues, and the need for help desks. As schools began to offer their first courses, they became very interested in shared systems that would lower their startup costs. The CTDLC stepped in to help, offering a shared infrastructure at an inexpensive price. Institutions were then able to focus on recruiting faculty, identifying courses and programs for development, and adjusting incentives, processes, and policies.

We have recently begun to offer new services to participating institutions. E-learning is now an option for many degree seekers, and it offers a wealth of opportunities to those who seek quality and convenience at a low price. To stay competitive, our member schools are collaborating around best practices and aiming to improve all their offerings—on ground and online—using the tools and strategies forged by online pedagogy.

I don't want to leave the impression that collaboration is easy or automatic—quite the contrary. Bringing stakeholders together to talk about collective approaches to shared problems takes time, resources, leadership, and the ability to get the right people in the room. The CTDLC has learned all these lessons the hard way, but we have clawed our way to success, and our many partners are cautiously optimistic about our future ventures. Success breeds future success, even if collaboration is risky. The CTDLC staff is asked to consult about collaboration almost as often as they are asked to consult about distance learning (Klonoski, 2001b).

As the distance learning landscape has shifted, so have the collaborative efforts of the CTDLC. Most schools that offer distance learning programs have created ongoing faculty training efforts—often as part of a learning center or similar institutional structure—that address the technical elements associated with online technologies and online pedagogies, such as how to manage a threaded discussion or create meaningful student interactions. There are assessment strategies for online learners just as there are other institutional assessments. For now, however, our distance learning growth rates have dropped from 70% per year to about 10%–20%. The tools of online delivery have been adopted by the entire academy as learning management systems (LMS), adding price, technical complexity, and increased uptime pressure to the delivery toolset. It requires real capital to launch an online program now, so schools must create specific business plans and strategies based on a serious evaluation of the market. Online programs must also provide student services to a dispersed population. The collaborative efforts of the CTDLC have shifted to LMS hosting, instructional design services (otherwise known as faculty training), web application development (i.e., online student services and systems integration), and distance learning management services.

One of the draws of a collaborative project is that you can break down its individual elements and outsource them. Take instructional design, for example. When an institution hires an instructional designer, it is paying for 40 hours of the designer's energy and technical skills. But when an institution outsources its instructional design work to an entire company, the company gets the specific hours it needs, not to mention the collective skill set of an entire instructional design group. (The same argument applies to LMS hosting.) As the complexity and cost of delivery systems increases, it is becoming impossible for small to midsized schools to afford (in terms of hardware and human talent) to operate them. Aggregating delivery costs around the LMS needs of several institutions spreads the pain and increases the resources available to operate these systems (Klonoski, 2005).

When an institution's leaders are trying to decide whether to collaborate with others on a particular activity, they should ask themselves two questions:

- Is this activity part of the core mission of our institution?

- Are we better served by learning to do this ourselves?

If the answer to both questions is "no," then an institution may either decide to collaborate or outsource. In one case, the CTDLC created a shared e-tutoring platform that allowed institutions to pool their tutoring talent, then extend tutor availability to off-site students. This collaborative approach allowed schools to expand tutor availability to nights and weekends without hiring additional help. In fact, the 16 schools sharing our system all elected to use each other's tutors, with some CTDLC-supplied training. They ultimately decided that sharing did not eliminate their competitive advantages or put their reputations at risk.

International online program development is another area that is rich with collaborative possibilities. Delivering U.S. educational programs in other countries requires solid relationships, trust, flexible pricing, cultural accommodation and awareness, and multilingual materials. Opportunities such as these are growing as Asia's economic engine picks up speed; organizations that learn how to collaborate and find mutual advantages for both parties will reap the rewards. This is not an area in which the CTDLC is working, but it is one that will definitely require collaborative approaches. We look forward to discovering these.

Online programs are already accelerating their progress toward shared degree offerings. As students discover that they can find online courses at institutions X and Y to fulfill their degree requirements at institution Z, they will start to demand that their home institution loosen its rules about residency and make course articulation transparent. If students point out that a course is not available at their home institution, or argue (with their parents) that the costs of a strict residency requirement are getting in the way, schools will soon learn that they must work to guarantee an efficient path toward degree completion if they want loyal alumni. Again, such an approach will result in institutions that see each other as partners, not competitors. As educational enterprises continue to confront questions about their core competencies, missions, and revenue needs, collaborating will help them become vastly more efficient.

Ed Klonoski is the executive director of the Connecticut Distance Learning Consortium.

The collaborations mentioned in the previous essay involved a broad set of players that worked together to accomplish great results, save money, and do more together than they could have done on their own. Yet none of the examples addressed the question of what happens when several campuses share one group of students. Several years ago, the University of Texas launched its TeleCampus. The TeleCampus coordinated the development of an online multicampus MBA degree program. The campuses devised the curriculum together, and each took responsibility for the development and delivery of two courses. Students could take classes from up to eight different campuses without regard to where their home base was. The difficulties behind the scenes were not easy to overcome, but the TeleCampus staff sorted them out as they arose. Since then, several more multicampus programs have developed, and the University of Texas TeleCampus has become an important asset to the system and to the state.

As Kansas State University's Virginia Moxley and Sue Maes explain in the following essay, an even more ambitious project, involving multiple campuses in multiple states, was developed at around the same time as TeleCampus. The institutions involved in the consortium were all land-grant universities, located (roughly) in the middle of the United States. The fact that the consortium became such a success reveals some interesting lessons.

The Great Plains IDEA Story
Virginia Moxley and Sue Maes

In 1994 the Great Plains Interactive Distance Education Alliance (Great Plains IDEA) was formed by a collegial group of human sciences academic deans who shared a common interest in educating rural professionals using distance courses. More than a decade later Great Plains IDEA has become a premier post-baccalaureate distance education provider that supports interinstitutional master's degrees and graduate certificates.

The alliance is made up of 10 research universities: Colorado State University, Iowa State University, Kansas State University, Michigan State University, Montana State University, North Dakota State University, Oklahoma State University, South Dakota State University, Texas Tech University, and the University of Nebraska. Its board of directors is composed of the dean or associate dean of the human sciences college at each of these partner universities. The alliance contracts with one of the participating universities to provide alliance management services.

The interinstitutional programs currently sponsored by the alliance include master's degrees and post-baccalaureate certificates in family financial planning, youth development, gerontology, merchandising, and community development. Additional programs are being developed. Great Plains IDEA students complete the interinstitutional programs entirely online. Most students hold down professional careers while also pursuing their graduate degrees.

The alliance began as an idea—a modest idea. The College of Human Resources and Family Sciences at the University of Nebraska had implemented its own distance education master's degree program and convened a meeting of Great Plains–area human sciences deans to determine whether any other institution had distance education graduate courses that might be available for use by their students. They also invited the other institutions to enroll their students in University of Nebraska courses.

The meeting stoked the competitive and cooperative tendencies of the participants. A new benchmark for graduate program access had been set, and no participant wanted the college he or she led to be behind the curve. But in the early years, there were major obstacles: a lack of Internet connectivity for rural professionals (the target demographic), an absence of commercially available and easy-to-use instructional software, and a paucity of distance education experience on the part of the faculty.

Early alliance initiatives focused on informing faculty about the changing marketplace for graduate education, showing them how to use technology to promote graduate learning at a distance, and developing a marketplace for shared distance education courses. At an online teaching seminar during those early years, one of the participating faculty members proposed that he and his colleagues team up to offer an interinstitutional master's program. Six months later, the interinstitutional faculty team met to develop their first program, in family financial planning.

The team began by developing a curriculum and dividing up teaching responsibilities. Then they got frustrated. There was no way the plan could comply with existing graduate school policies, not to mention the fact that the credit transfer process seemed unduly expensive and complicated. Worse, the cost to students varied widely from course to course, depending on the policies at the host university. As good as the curriculum was, no member of the planning team was convinced that he or she could sell the idea to departmental colleagues or graduate program administrators back home.

The academic administrators reviewed the work of the faculty team and created a strategy to manage the most frustrating conundrums presented by the proposal. They then began the process of informing faculty and administration at their home institutions about the plan to offer an interinstitutional program. Their conversations touched on the problems that had to be solved prior to implementation, but they also revealed that the solution lay with people the academic administrator did not oversee: graduate deans, chief financial officers, continuing education administrators, and registrars. These groups were soon engaged in the planning process.

The graduate deans developed principles that would guide their institutions' participation in the Great Plains IDEA post-baccalaureate programs. Adherence to these deceptively simple principles would later prove essential to the programs' success. They required that partners in the interinstitutional program treat each other as equals (e.g., graduate faculty status at one partner institution would be honored by all partners), respect institutional differences (e.g., faculty workload, institutional administration, course numbers and degree titles would be institutional prerogatives), and simplify student navigation (e.g., the student's home university would provide administrative and support services).

After thoroughly reviewing and analyzing the cost and price of online education at the partner universities, the chief financial officers recommended that all students enrolled in courses sponsored by the alliance pay the same price. (Although all of the participating institutions would charge the same amount, the ratio of tuition to fees did vary from state to state.) The officers further recommended that the proceeds from these courses be distributed accordingly: 75% to the teaching university, 12.5% to the student's home university, and 12.5% in support of the alliance. Once again, a deceptively simple solution—agreeing on a common price—took care of a number of vexing problems.

The registrars and graduate and academic deans agreed that students would enroll in interinstitutional courses by registering at their home universities. Students would be taught by faculty from all participating universities and could study with other schools' students, too. The transfer of academic records would be facilitated by a secure interinstitutional database, which would be managed by each university's program coordinators. The programs' outcomes assessment plan and reports would be centrally supported; each school would be given access.

The Great Plains IDEA is a joint project of its member universities. It sponsors interinstitutional programs, but does not admit students to the programs or award degrees. Only the partner universities can admit students who meet the appropriate criteria and award degrees to those who meet program and institutional requirements.

The Great Plains IDEA has proven to be so functional that other groups have adopted the model. Its web site (www.gpidea.org)

includes information about the interinstitutional programs sponsored by the alliance and links to its partner universities for more in-depth program information. The web site also features a collaboration resource center that provides information about the alliance and its policies and practices.

Virginia Moxley is a founding member and past board chair of the Great Plains IDEA and is interim dean of the Kansas State University College of Human Ecology. Sue Maes is senior development officer for the Educational Communications Center at Kansas State University. Moxley and Maes codirect Kansas State University's Institute for Academic Alliances.

Staff who developed and operate the Great Plains IDEA have been helping other groups of institutions that are ready to combine their resources to enable them to offer more choices to their local students. While it is never simple to coordinate institutional systems that were designed to serve only local needs, the Great Plains IDEA is proof that it can be done.

Helping Faculty Work Together

In the mid 1990s a unique type of consortium was developed. Realizing that electronic materials were time consuming to create (but vital to have), its founders developed a way for faculty members to share their materials, or "learning objects," and get credit at their home institutions for doing so. The story that Gerry Hanley tells about managing this complex organization is interesting and enlightening. You will see that the success of any consortium lies, in part, with its members' ability to communicate with each other.

Reaching Outside Your Campus to Bring Solutions Inside: The Collaborative Proposition of MERLOT for Higher Education
Gerard L. Hanley

Developing the MERLOT Collaborative

MERLOT (Multimedia Educational Resource for Learning and Online Teaching; see www.merlot.org) was created in 1997 to serve faculty members' growing need to incorporate high-quality online resources into their courses. In the early years, the cost, timeliness, and reliability of developing high-quality online instructional materials were key challenges in attaining the California State University Integrated Technology Strategy's outcomes. MERLOT was designed to be a web-based digital library for academic and technological communities—a place where the communities could share their online learning and teaching materials.

As other university systems became aware of MERLOT, they began to recognize the value of working together to increase their institutions' opportunities. In 1998 the University System of Georgia, the Oklahoma State Regents for Higher Education, the University of North Carolina system, and the California State University system created an informal consortium that represented almost 100 campuses and served more than 900,000 students and more than 47,000 faculty. The State Higher Education Executive Officers organization (SHEEO) coordinated the cooperative of these four state systems. By 1999 each of them had realized that they could expand the MERLOT collections, conduct peer reviews of digital learning materials, and contribute student learning assignments. Each system contributed $20,000 to develop the MERLOT software and more than $30,000 in in-kind support to advance the collaborative project. The California State University (CSU) maintained leadership of and responsibility for the operation and the improvement of its processes and tools. In January 2000 the four systems each sponsored 12 faculty members (from the disciplines of biology, physics, business, and teacher education) in developing evaluation standards and peer review processes for online teaching and learning material. Today, MERLOT has 16 higher education system partners, 10 campus partners, 13 professional society partners, 9 digital library partners, and 19 corporate partners and sponsors (see http://taste.merlot.org/participating/partner/all_list.htm for details). CSU continues to provide leadership and significant support for the MERLOT project in service of worldwide higher education.

Managing the MERLOT Collaborative

There are four intersecting communities in the MERLOT collaborative that require management to sustain their growth and value to members: an institutional stakeholder community, a disciplinary community, a professional development community, and an individual user community.

Institutional stakeholder community. MERLOT is now a consortium of institutional stakeholder communities, including higher education institutions, professional societies, digital library organizations, and corporations. MERLOT manages the collaboration between its partners in the institutional community through a participation agreement and an active project directors' council. The participation agreement defines what institutions will give and receive when they join the collaborative. MERLOT provides technology, consultation, a faculty development curriculum, peer review training, and free registration to the MERLOT International Conference. It also offers institutions the opportunity to take part in planning and evaluating MERLOT's strategic and operational direction. In return the institutional partners agree to contribute funds, support conferences, and provide in-kind support to faculty participating in peer review and training. They further agree to integrate MERLOT into their institutional initiatives (for more details, see MERLOT, 2005–2006). One of the top priorities of the MERLOT administrative team is to facilitate the collaborative's decision-making processes while developing and managing operations to achieve the strategic and tactical goals defined by the project directors' council.

The collaborative proposition for higher education has been that making financial and in-kind contributions to a well-managed cooperative can produce timely, institutionally valued services of high quality. The scope of services that MERLOT provides would not have been possible for institutions to offer individually, so it was vital that all participating systems agree to cooperate with one another. Their regular communication with each other and their participation in the management of the collaborative have enabled MERLOT to sustain and develop its services, which further supports its communities. MERLOT continues to add value with new initiatives in workforce development, institutional teaching commons, and its integration into learning management systems (e.g., Blackboard, WebCT, Angel Learning, and Desire2Learn).

Disciplinary communities. One of MERLOT's core services is its peer review of online materials. Its institutional partners support their faculty by participating on MERLOT's 15 editorial boards, which evaluate the quality of content, pedagogical soundness, and usability of more than 13,000 online materials in the MERLOT collection. Each of these boards consists of faculty from a relatively well-defined disciplines (e.g., physics, business, music, etc.) who are volunteering or are supported in their contributions by the institutional partners. There are two aspects to managing collaboration within the editorial boards: the management of peer review work within a discipline, as performed by faculty worldwide, and the management of the quality and reliability of the peer review process across discipline-based editorial boards. MERLOT helps manage the multidisciplinary peer review process by establishing official policies and training, dividing up the work, and recognizing contributions by editorial board members. There are more than 250 faculty peer reviewers, and the MERLOT administrative team manages a personnel evaluation procedure so that faculty members and their supporting institutions receive recognition for their important contributions to teaching and learning with technology. The team also conducts monthly conference calls with editors and meets face to face three times a year to review and revise policies and technologies used to fulfill its mission. To manage the peer review work within the discipline-based editorial boards, MERLOT developed a sophisticated workflow technology that enhances efficiency and accountability. The members of the editorial boards meet face to face once a year at the MERLOT International Conference, but also take part in monthly conference calls. Disciplinary portals recommend ways to use technology when teaching individual subjects. By staying visible, the disciplinary community continually (and publicly) reinforces its identity.

Managing the editorial boards with one eye on the needs of faculty members has been key to MERLOT's success with disciplinary communities. The editorial boards have been invigorated by their ability to deliver services that enhance teachers' overall success. This has been a unique and very positive experience for MERLOT faculty leaders. In addition, the consortium gives faculty a chance to engage in dialogue and decision-making on a national and multidisciplinary scale—a leadership opportunity they may not have on their own campus. All these things motivate faculty to participate in and lead the MERLOT disciplinary communities. The consortium gives them an opportunity to surmount barriers to cooperation in a way that may be difficult to do at their own institutions.

Professional development communities. Campus-based leaders who want to change teaching and learning practices within a relatively stable academic culture must develop the skills, knowledge, and attitudes of faculty to successfully use technology to improve education. Many campus positions provide this opportunity, including director of faculty development, director of teaching and

learning centers, director of academic technology services, director
of libraries, and chief information officer. MERLOT provides a curriculum and professional development training to its community
partners, enabling campuses to use previously tested materials to
plan training, conduct workshops, and customize their services.
These offerings are designed to help institutions to reliably, quickly,
and successfully implement MERLOT services in an institutional
context. MERLOT's structured forums include conferences, workshops, training, and curricula, all of which serve as catalysts for collaboration among institutional and disciplinary communities.

Community of individual members. MERLOT's collection of
online materials, comments, assignments, personal contributions,
and teaching cases has been contributed by faculty, students, staff,
librarians, administrators, and other members of the worldwide
MERLOT community. The individual objects on MERLOT's electronic "shelves" are determined by its members' judgment about
what materials are important to share with their colleagues. There is
no charge for anonymous users to search, browse, and find online
materials in MERLOT, but there is also no charge to become an
individual, registered member and use certain services. Members
who want to contribute their work or expertise to MERLOT can
register and fill out forms on the Internet. Individuals who have created member profiles automatically are provided with an online
portfolio of their contributions. MERLOT stays in step with academic culture by always associating a person's name with his or her
contributions to the community collection. In a one month period
(March 2006), more than 250 new materials were contributed by
MERLOT members, and approximately 900 new individuals
joined the MERLOT community. MERLOT remains active and
continues to grow.

MERLOT enables communication between its four communities through an internal listserv newsletter, *From the Vineyard,* and
an external newsletter, *The Grapevine.* These communities are con-

nected within a shared framework that validates and supports the differing needs of faculty, faculty developers, and administrators, and has played an important part in sustaining collaboration since 2000. MERLOT's cause is championed by all of its leaders, including project directors (about 25 campus administrative leaders), editorial board members (about 250 faculty leaders), and individual members (more than 33,000). With the equivalent of just nine full-time staff on its administrative team, MERLOT requires hundreds of thousands of collaborators to fulfill its mission.

Gerard L. Hanley is the executive director of MERLOT (Multimedia Educational Resource for Learning and Online Teaching) at the California State University Office of the Chancellor.

In short, MERLOT is a highly managed consortium whose communities are relatively autonomous but whose work is leveraged to advance each community's mission. The main responsibility of the MERLOT administrative team is to understand the needs of different communities and design services to satisfy those needs in a cost-effective and timely fashion. By reaching beyond local campuses and systems, and participating in larger collaboratives like MERLOT, you may be able to find solutions to your own school's problems. Institutions that share their expertise, risk, and resources within a well-managed collaborative can bring "outside" solutions "inside" as accepted practices.

What Are the Lessons We Can Learn From These Institutional Consortia?

As the previous stories demonstrate, you can accomplish more working with others than you can on your own, whether you're pooling funds to get better deals on products or services, or sharing faculty across multiple campuses to enrich local programs. Of course, none of these things can be accomplished without a lot of effort. Ed Klonoski's question about whether to join in a consortial effort is an important one. When you start wondering if your institution could potentially outsource or share its resources, you must ask yourself if these activities would reflect the core mission of the institution. It is also vital to determine whether the overall health of your institution is better served by having staff members learn to develop and manage activities themselves or by joining with others. Collaborating means giving up some control over your activities—but, as we have seen with the Great Plains IDEA project, safeguards can be built in to ensure quality.

As University of Alaska president Mark Hamilton recently put it when announcing the formation of a statewide collaborative project, working together is a lose-lose proposition. If we had all the resources we desired, we would design the exact products and services that we need. But we do not have unlimited resources. In a consortium, you may not get exactly what your institution or organization wants, but you are more likely to get something that will fit your needs than you would on your own. Working with others requires compromise, but sometimes those compromises result in better services—for everyone.

Failures

It is good to learn from positive examples, but also useful to understand why some collaborative efforts have failed. There have been a few rather public partnership failures. One was the United Kingdom's eUniversities Worldwide (U.K. eU). This project was launched in 2000 with the idea that traditional universities could share marketing and technological resources to reach worldwide audiences with distance learning services. By late April 2004, however, the board of the Higher Education Funding Council for England announced it was pulling the project's funding. Although approximately 900 students had registered before UK eU ceased operations, this was not enough to satisfy the project's backers.

There is a lot of speculation about why this alliance failed. An April 2004 news article posted on the Observatory on Borderless Higher

Education (http://www.obhe.ac.uk) noted that it could have been bad timing: The U.K. eU emerged at about the same time as the dot-com bust. The project also seemed to have been funded as a reaction to what universities in other countries were already doing, rather than being based on any empirically supported estimate of worldwide need or interest in online courses from English universities. In addition, U.K. eU managers made the very expensive decision to create their own course management system instead of working with one that was available to buy or lease. Ultimately, it may have been that U.K. eU's backers expected much faster results than were possible. The original business model may have predicted thousands of students within the first two years, but these forecasts did not match reality. Still, if creating partnerships were easy, there would be no failures (Johnstone, Conger, Bernath, Husson, Maurandi, & Perez de Madrigal, 2005).

New Breed of Collaborations

Open Educational Resources (OER) is another movement that has emerged as a worldwide force and has been endorsed by the United Nations Educational, Cultural, and Scientific Organization (UNESCO).[1] OER's mission is to create and grant access to learning and teaching resources, and those that ensure the quality of education and educational practices. Learning resources include courseware, content modules, learning objects, learner support and assessment tools, and online learning communities. Teaching resources include tools and support materials for creating, adapting, and using OER, as well as training materials and other teaching tools. The concept of OER champions the global sharing of knowledge as a way to increase human intellectual capacity.

This is a wonderful goal, and many in higher education are excited by the idea of sharing their work with others around the world. But how can OER help individual campuses? When speaking at a recent university forum, I tried to explain OER to a group of professors. I began by referencing MIT's OpenCourseWare (see http://ocw.mit.edu) project, which allows anyone to have access to the materials used in almost 2,000 MIT courses. (For most courses, that includes a syllabus, lecture notes, readings, recitations, labs, assignments, exams, projects, and other related materials.) The following day I ran into one of the professors from the forum. He stopped me and explained that he had tried out the MIT materials. It seems he was teaching an online statistics course and there was one part of the course that made him uncomfortable every time he taught it. He went to the MIT web site and looked at how their faculty presented the same concept. He literally ripped the section he wanted and mixed it into his own course. This whole process took place while he watched a sporting event on television.

Thanks to the support and vision of the education staff at the William and Flora Hewlett Foundation (see www.hewlett.org), there are now 36 institutions in 11 countries that have active open courseware sites. (Another 35 institutions have projects in early stages of development.) A host of open content projects allows for similarly collaborative endeavors, including Rice University's Connexions platform (see http://cnx.rice.edu), which helps create a repository of course materials from many subject areas and provides users with free software to ensure compatibility. Authors license their materials through Creative Commons (see Chapter 4, www.creativecommons.org) and are linked with one another through open communities, which allows them to get help and feedback from other users. This project takes the collaborative concept behind MERLOT (highlighted earlier in this chapter) to new levels.

Even as I write this, I am involved in a multiweek virtual forum hosted by UNESCO that focuses on what research needs to be done better to use and create OERs. By exchanging simple emails, dozens of participants from Europe, North America, Africa, and the Asia-Pacific region are trading ideas on how to proceed with OER expansion. As you might expect, hot topics include issues of quality, the collaborative creation of materials, and the best technological and curricular applications of these materials. A researcher from the Organisation for Economic Co-operation and Development (OECD; www.oecd.org) recently mentioned that in his first attempt to gauge the scope of OER activities in higher education, his team sent out more than 1,800 emails to university administrators in 30 countries, they received only 14 responses (J. Hylén, personal communication, March, 2006). Those of us on the advisory group for that study suggested that a top-down approach might not work. In many respects, OER still seems to be a grassroots activity—and institutional management may not be aware of it in their schools. In any case, because of the poor response rate, OECD developed a new survey that targeted individual users and developers of OER. After just a month on the project's web site, the survey had garnered 160 responses.

In this new world of educational materials development, the face of collaboration has changed. It may exist outside a traditional educational framework, but its materials are used by students and educators. Communities of interested people come together in self-selected groups to create and share these resources online. Wikipedia is one prominent example. Some may argue with the validity of its materials, but the online encyclopedia is an amazing resource. For the students of the Net generation, or digital natives, it is the first place to look for information. We should learn from its online community of people who care enough about specific subjects to write articles and contribute them to the world. Chapter 7 explores the use of such online communities as educational tools.

Policy and Collaboration

Since we know that faculty and students collaborate in the creation and use of online materials, and that collaboration has become a significant way to create new knowledge, we need to consider how institutional policies support or hinder these activities. Some consortia will try to incorporate traditional campus practices in their efforts to encourage participation, but most will not. Unfortunately, there is no easy way to separate favorable policies from unfavorable ones. In previous chapters, we have suggested that periodic policy audits may be a good idea. We have also stressed the importance of having strong policies on intellectual property and making sure the entire campus knows and respects those policies.

In an era when ICTs are both mandatory and expensive for campuses, it is critical for institutions of higher education to learn how they can work together to accomplish their goals. The outsourcing of important (but nonacademic) services like food preparation, bookstore sales, and dormitory management has become commonplace. Dealing with areas that have a more immediate connection to academic services requires even more involvement on the part of the campus community. Figuring out which services or activities are worthy candidates for collaboration, and deciding which organizations to collaborate with, is only part of the hard work. Changing staff members' thinking about why they do what they do takes just as much planning and effort.

As previously noted, it is important for institutional and academic leaders to ensure that the policies designed to govern practices and activities pre-Internet do not get in the way of new, innovative projects. I am not suggesting that we throw out all the old policies, but we do need to raise questions when practical attempts to share certain academic and nonacademic services don't work. The policies that govern those services need to be examined.

If your institution decides to engage in collaborative activities, you may want to develop some new policy guidelines. Also, the reward structure for faculty and staff should include some recognition of their collaborative activities. As more and more consortia evolve, it may be useful to think about interinstitutional collaboration guidelines, which could include:

- Tips on finding appropriate collaboration partners

- Models of formal agreements that could be used when first developing partnerships, which could contain information on the resources being contributed and those being accepted

- Information on the levels and types of interactions that are needed among partners (the advice on this score is "there can never be too much")

Here is some general advice on sustaining collaborations (provided by my colleague, William Husson in Johnstone et al., 2005):

- Never sacrifice quality, but be sure you can distinguish quality from "doing things the way we always have."

- Build internal coalitions and communicate with your colleagues so no one reads about your project for the first time in the newspaper.

- Be meticulous about staying within the regulations of your government, state, province, and/or accrediting body (but see if they will stretch).

- Realize that collaborations only work when all parties and students win.

One thing we do know: Collaborations work best when they fulfill a real need that is recognized by everyone involved. When this happens, each participant becomes more motivated to solve whatever problems come along. When you are ready to start forming your own partnerships, do not underestimate how vital it is to keep communicating. The more areas in which you have partners, the more you will be able to accomplish for your students (and the fewer resources you will need).

Summing Up

Colleges and universities are finding ways to do things together, because they must. Whether the collaborations are organized through statewide higher education systems, common affiliations (e.g., JesuitNet, land-grant universities), or campus connections, we have learned some lessons about making them work. We must partner with others to make our resources go as far as possible, but forming collaborative relationships among institutions uses another precious resource: time. It is critical for institutional leaders to assess the efficacy of any partnerships that evolve. Those that are likely to serve the mission and goals of their institutions are the only ones worth pursuing. They are the ones that will ultimately become most sustainable and valuable to the campus.

Endnote

1) The OER term was first defined at UNESCO's 2002 *Forum on the Impact of Open Courseware for Higher Education in Developing Countries.* OER was further refined at UNESCO's 2004 *Second Global Forum on International Quality Assurance, Accreditation and the Recognition of Qualifications in Higher Education.* In 2005, UNESCO's International Institute for Educational Planning hosted a six-week international electronic forum on OER to uncover the issues associated with helping the OER movement expand.

References

Capriccioso, R. (2006). Stem cells meet Google. *Inside Higher Ed.* Retrieved July 14, 2006, from: http://insidehighered.com/news /2006/03/08/coleman

Epper, R. M., & Garn, M. (2003). *Virtual college and university consortia: A national study.* Boulder, CO: SHEEO

Johnstone, S. M., & Conger, S. B., with Bernath, U., Husson, W. J., Maurandi, A. L., & Perez de Madrigal, M. E. (2005). Strategic alliances: Collaboration for sustainability. In A. Hope & P. Guiton (Eds.), *Strategies for sustainable open and distance learning* (pp. 111–130). New York, NY: Routledge.

Klonoski, Ed. (2001a, March/April). e-Lobbying: Marketing e-learning to the legislature. *The Technology Source.* Retrieved July 18, 2006, from: http://technologysource.org/article/elobbying/

Klonoski, Ed. (2001b). Consortial IT services: Collaborating to reduce the pain. *EDUCAUSE Quarterly 24*(2), 28–33.

Klonoski, Ed. (2005, April/May). Cost-saving collaboration: Purchasing and deploying a statewide learning management system. *Innovate: Journal of Online Education, 1*(4). Retrieved July 18, 2006, from: http://www.innovateonline.info/index.php?view=article&id=69

MERLOT. (2005–2006). *System partner application for freshman year participation in MERLOT.* Retrieved July 17, 2006, from: http://taste .merlot.org/participating/partner/system_app05-06.pdf

7 ··· Putting It All Together

Sally M. Johnstone

America's universities bear some uncomfortable resemblances to Detroit's big three carmakers in the 1950s: General Motors, Ford, and Chrysler also presumed they would always rule the roost.

—*"Remember Detroit," 2006*

This dire analogy describes the competitiveness of U.S. higher education in the world marketplace, but it could also be used to illustrate the complacency of many people at colleges and universities. Even with budget cuts and negative public demands, students are still coming to our campuses. In some states there are fewer coming than in others, but the reality is that things are not terrible on most campuses—yet. My concern is that the usual inertia associated with campuses may ultimately be a big problem, considering that the rest of our students' lives (and those of their parents) are changing very fast. We no longer have the luxury of debating whether we should do things differently or adopt new tools. Instead, campus communities must start now to plan *how* they will adapt.

In previous chapters, we have introduced you to the ways in which many colleges and universities have begun this process of adaptation. We have also included some negative examples, in order to keep you from repeating those mistakes. I believe that those of us who work in American higher education have the creativity and will to face any challenge. Given that, I'd like to push your thinking a little further. The following essay should make us all consider ways to think more openly when guiding higher education to the next level.

The Role of Openness in the Future of Higher Education
David Wiley

As detailed in popular publications like Thomas L. Friedman's (2005) *The World Is Flat,* the world is changing in many ways. Some sectors, such as business and science, have used change to their benefit. Others, including academia, have adapted very little in response to change and are consequently in danger of becoming irrelevant. Of the many shifts that are occurring, at least six are worth considering in the context of the future of higher education (see Table 7.1).

Business, science, and life are rapidly moving toward digitization, openness, and the other indicators in the "To" column, while higher education continues to languish in the "From" column. There is an increasingly sharp distinction between the learning that today's students do inside the classroom and that which takes place outside the classroom. A typical higher education class might proceed as follows: Students are inside a classroom (tethered to a place), using textbooks and handouts (printed materials). They must pay tuition and register to attend this class (the experience is closed). Talking during class or working with others outside of class is generally discouraged (each student is isolated, though surrounded by peers), and each student receives exactly the same instruction (the information presented is generic). Students are students (consumers); they do not participate in the teaching process.

Now compare that classroom learning experience to a possible learning experience outside the classroom. From a dorm room, student center, coffee shop, or even a bus, a student connects to the Internet using a laptop (students are mobile), then uses www.google.com to find a relevant web page (accessing an open digital resource). While carrying out this search, the student chats with friends on the phone and instant messages others to see if they have any relevant information (students are connected to other people). The students follow

Table 7.1
Changes Occurring Business, Science, and the World

From	To	Examples
Analog/Print	Digital	Voice-over-IP (VoIP), e-books, digital newspapers (e.g., *New York Times*, *Washington Post*)
Closed	Open	Open source software, open access weather and astronomical data, Public Library of Science journals
Tethered	Mobile	Batteries in laptops, cell phones, wireless Internet access
Isolated	Connected	Email, instant messaging, hypertext, web services, and other interconnected systems
Generic	Personal	Customized interiors for cars, skins and ring tones for cell phones, hard drives, RAM, and video components in computers
Consumption	Participation	News, radio, movies spawned by blogs, podcasting, and video podcasting

links from one web site to another, explores related pages (content is connected to other content), ignores irrelevant material (students get what is important to them personally), and quickly finds what he or she needs. The student shares his or her finds with friends by phone and instant message (students participate in the teaching process).

A similarly digital, open, mobile, connected, personal, participatory story could be told about a day in the life of an engineer or researcher. As life, business, and science drift further away from higher education, how can we continue to add value to the lives of those who pour their hearts, souls, years, and dollars into education? What is higher education's value proposition? This question is worth considering.

Once upon a time, college and university courses were the primary repositories of postsecondary curricular content. Today, initiatives like OpenCourseWare provide content seekers from around the world with a legitimate alternative source of curricular materials.

Once upon a time, the university library was the primary repository of research. Its archives contained peer-reviewed journals, monographs, and more. Today, initiatives like the Public Library of Science and preprint services like www.arXiv.org provide individuals from around the world with a legitimate alternative source of research.

Once upon a time, a college or university's faculty was the primary repository of technical and academic knowledge in a community. Today, technologies like email and instant messaging almost instantly put seekers of expertise in touch with faculty at many universities, as well as professionals, "pro-am" hobbyists, and others around the world.

Once upon a time, the degree programs of our colleges and universities were the credentials most highly valued by employers. Today, certification as a Microsoft Certified Systems Engineer, Cisco Certified Internetwork Expert, or Red Hat Certified Architect may be worth more to an employer than a four-year degree in computer science.

Once upon a time, higher education enjoyed a monopoly on curricular content, research archives, expertise, and credentialing. Each of these monopolies has been broken in the recent past, but our institutions have yet to recognize and respond to these changes in their environment.

What should higher education do? On the surface, offering distance education courses seems like a reasonable idea. But are online classes the answer? In short, no.

Table 7.2 highlights some features of an average online course.

Table 7.2
Characteristics of an Online Course

Analog/Print	**Digital**
Closed	Open
Tethered	**Mobile**
Isolated	Connected
Generic	Personal
Consumption	Participation

While it is true that the materials in an online course are digital, and can therefore be accessed and used by many people (in many locations) at the same time, online courses meet just two of the six criteria that higher education need to stay aligned with business, science, and life in general. Online courses require tuition, registration, and passwords (they are closed), and are notoriously more socially isolating than face-to-face courses. They provide digital copies of the same lecture notes and activities to all students (they are generic), and place students in the position of simply downloading materials (they make them the ultimate consumers).

We must recognize that it is not only "the world" that is changing, but also our students' lives. Today's undergraduates are accustomed to instant, on-demand access to multiple people and sources of information via myriad technologies. Walk into any teenager's bedroom and you will see him or her watching a DVD, listening to music, surfing the web, talking on the phone, and instant messaging a few friends, all at the same time. Is it any wonder that students who can simultaneously manage and filter multiple channels of synchronous and asynchronous information tend to find a 60-minute lecture difficult to tolerate?

Significant societal changes are occurring that affect students' lives. Higher education must take an innovative approach to teaching and learning if it is to remain relevant.

How is higher education to respond to this changing environment and the changing nature of its core offerings: content, research, expertise, and credentialing? E-learning (at least as commonly conceived) is not the answer. Instead, the university experience must more closely reflect society. Higher education must continue its efforts to become digital and mobile, while working to become significantly more open, connected, personal, and participatory.

In an attempt to make higher education more innovative, we might ask a professor to demonstrate certain behaviors in the classroom, such as using a problem-based approach, or having students work in small teams. But the diversity in teachers' and learners' levels of preparation and backgrounds, combined with the differences in the academic disciplines themselves, makes it impossible to conscionably recommend these or any other teaching techniques for universal application in higher education. Still, there is an innovative teaching and learning strategy that can be applied broadly, to the great benefit of higher education and all of its stakeholders. That strategy is openness.

I believe that the movement toward greater openness in education, as exemplified by programs such as the OpenCourseWare (OCW) initiatives (currently in use at the Massachusetts Institute of Technology [MIT], Johns Hopkins University, Tufts University, University of Notre Dame, Utah State University, Foothill-De Anza Community College, and the Utah College of Applied Technology) is one of the truly great teaching and learning innovations of the last several decades. I believe that openness is the gateway to connectedness, personalization, and participation, and that it is a catalyst for further innovation.

Consider the following examples:

- As a faculty member, if I want to create review or remediation opportunities for students by connecting my course materials to the prerequisite materials they have studied, my students and I need access to these materials. Without openness, the level of connectivity my students desire is not attainable.

- As a faculty member, if I want to personalize the experience for my students—or, more important, if I want to empower my students to meaningfully personalize the experience for themselves—the materials we use must be customizable. Without openness, nothing can be changed or adapted, and the level of personalization my students desire cannot be attained.

- As a faculty member, if I want to engage my students in creating and contributing resources, tutorials, and other study materials to a class, I can do so more easily with an open repository for course materials. Without this openness, there is no room for the students' contributions, and the degree of participation they desire will not be attainable.

We look to the Research I universities for innovations in research and teaching with good reason. Many members of the public consider these schools to be the very pinnacle of higher education. It may surprise you, then, to hear that when faculty at MIT, Utah State University, and other universities are invited to open up their syllabi, lecture notes, assignments, and other materials for consumption, some faculty members ask for time to "tidy up" first. They are cautious, because the move toward openness takes them directly into the heart of the scholarly world, exposing them to the quality-increasing pressures of the peer review. Their materials then become open to other kinds of review, as they demonstrate an unprecedented level of transparency to higher education stakeholders (including parents and alumni).

Several recent reports already brought to the attention of the Commission on the Future of Higher Education, such as *Innovate America* and *Rising Above the Gathering Storm,* have indicated the absolute urgency with which the U.S. must work to develop, recruit, and retain the best and brightest students (from home and abroad) to study science and engineering. Recent analyses (Carson, 2006) of evaluation data from MIT OCW show that 35% of freshmen who were aware of OCW prior to attending MIT indicate that the site was a significant or very significant influence on their choice of school. This number is up from 8% the year before. The world's best and brightest students already see openness as an incredible innovation capable of catalyzing further innovations, and they are beginning to include a commitment to openness in the list of criteria by which they select institutions.

The time will come when OpenCourseWare (or a similar collection of open-access educational materials) will be as common at institutions of higher education as informational web sites are now. The United States can either lead this charge (as we did with the previous generation of higher education web sites) or follow the rest of the world. There are already active consortia of universities engaged in OCW projects in China, Japan, and South America, with other efforts underway at individual universities in Europe and elsewhere. Considering the total number of universities that are actively involved, the U.S. is already behind. Our prime-mover advantage in this area, and our ability to attract top students, may not last long. We must broaden our commitment to openness in higher education and begin to innovate atop that platform.

It is commonly said with regard to large sections of general education courses that "everything past the fifth row of the auditorium is distance education." To some extent, this is true—techniques that work well for a 30-student course tend to deteriorate rapidly as the number of students increases to 50, 100, or 300. After a while, the value of our best pedagogical tools may seem to have vanished completely. What you may be amazed to find, however, is that the inverse is also true: Learning techniques that serve extremely large groups of students deteriorate just as rapidly when 10,000 becomes 2,000, 200, or 50. Higher education is largely unacquainted with this insight because until recently, it was impossible to imagine the members of such a large group communicating with each other at the same time.

There is much for us to learn by studying the social, linguistic, and political structures of very large online communities. These communities are a core part of the everyday experience of many of our students, and they are the models our students will compare us to in terms of openness, connectedness, personalization, and participation. As every good student knows, there is much to be learned from studying the grading rubric for an exam, and these large online communities may well hold the key to affordably scaling up our educational offerings while simultaneously aligning higher education with the rest of modern society. This is just one area that could be enhanced by a commitment to openness.

In summary, higher education has fallen out of step with business, science, and everyday life. In order to keep up with changes in society and our student populations, higher education must become an innovator in the areas of openness, connectedness, personalization, and participation. I believe that openness is the key to enabling other innovations and catalyzing improvements in the quality, accountability, affordability, and accessibility of higher education.

David Wiley is an associate professor at Utah State University and director of the Center for Open and Sustainable Learning. This essay is abstracted from his testimony given in February 2006 to the U.S. Secretary of Education's Commission on the Future of Higher Education. The full text is available on his web site: http://www.david-wiley.com

David's essay explains how to proceed in a world that is fully connected and how to serve students who have grown up in that world. He urges us to consider new ways of opening up our colleges and universities. But he also (accurately) points out that our usual attempts to expand access to our campuses through online courses and programs do not go very far in a new, connected, open world.

In previous chapters, I mentioned the open universities that evolved in various parts of the world when governments wanted their citizens to have greater access to an affordable postsecondary education. (This vision of "openness" is somewhat different from what David Wiley is talking about.) In March 2006 the Open University (OU) in the U.K. announced that it was creating an Open Content Initiative (OCI). The OCI "will make educational resources freely available on the Internet, with state-of-the-art learning support and collaboration tools to connect students and educators" (Open University, 2006, ¶ 3). As Brenda Gourley, vice chancellor of the Open University, put it:

> The philosophy of open access and sharing knowledge
> is a wonderful fit with the founding principles of The

Open University and with the University's very strong commitment to opening up educational access and widening participation. The University will be developing forms of open content e-learning which will reach less-experienced learners and, we hope, encourage an appetite for further learning. The Open University will be the first in the U.K. to offer Open Content materials under a Creative Commons license. We are deeply grateful to The William and Flora Hewlett Foundation for its generous support. (Open University, 2006, ¶ 5)

This project is especially remarkable because the OU's financial base is the development and "sale" of its course materials. The innovative staff at the OU is testing a business model that will allow them to contribute high-quality materials to an emerging open environment. Their efforts should give hope to all of the college and university planners who are ready to begin thinking about how their campuses can move in a new direction.

Outsourcing Semiacademic Services

As previously noted, things that were once done inside institutions of higher education can now be done at a lower cost by outside vendors. Most campuses do not create their own course management systems, but instead license externally produced software or incorporate open-source products. The way these tools work has a profound effect on how faculty members structure the teaching of their courses. They make it easier for online courses to include a wide variety of materials, but what can or cannot be included depends on the tool. We have discussed how faculty and students work together, touching on the fact that students are influenced and driven by forces outside an instructor's domain. We have also discussed the fact that the creation of electronic course materials by a single faculty member for his or her sole use is an inefficient use of institutional resources that frequently results in products that are not as good as they might otherwise be. The best course materials draw on many resources, but to be cost effective, they also need to be used by a large number of students—more than a single faculty member can usually manage.

In some cases it is easy to overcome this problem: Institutions can delegate some of the management tasks of teaching to teaching assistants. Unfortunately, there needs to be a pool of people willing and able to work in this capacity—and that is rarely the case at two- and four-year colleges. Consequently, new companies are forming to provide these services. One of the best known is Smarthinking, a prominent tutoring service that now helps teachers grade composition essays. Smarthinking's Grade Guidance program is staffed by people from around the world, all of whom have master's degrees or doctorates and are trained to evaluate written work according to rubrics supplied by individual colleges and universities. The company guarantees to return students' papers within 24 hours, with extensive comments included. This allows students to receive timely and intensive feedback on papers and essays that a single faculty member would be hard-pressed to provide.[1]

This type of outsourcing allows faculty members to teach a larger number of students per class without sacrificing quality. It also frees up their time to pay more attention to students who need special help. Institutions receive full grade reports and are able to establish a greater consistency in grading among different classes. To take this program a step further, Smarthinking is exploring methodologies that will allow them to incorporate technology into the grading process. Students' papers would first be reviewed by an automated grading system, then be given to people who would examine the machine's work and add their own comments. Automation would likely reduce costs, since—as has been noted throughout this book— higher education's biggest expense is its people. It is vital to look for ways for faculty to do what they do best, automating what we can without reducing the quality of students' learning.

This is not the only service that can be used by campuses to free up faculty time. But before choosing to outsource any service, one should thoroughly examine its benefits and disadvantages, looking at more than just the cost. Appropriate members of the campus community should be involved in these decisions. As noted before, when radical changes are to be implemented, it is critical to manage expectations and address resistance ahead of time. It will pay off in the long run.

What Can Campus Leaders Do?

All of the issues raised in this book need to be addressed, but not all at once. It takes many years to counter the inertia of "the-way-things-have-always-been-done." The exact starting point is different for each campus and depends on its internal culture. My advice is to always start by seeking the path of least resistance, but it also helps to make academic and nonacademic staff understand the problems at hand. Campus-wide colloquia that give all staff a chance to hear different perspectives on the challenges that face them can be useful starting places for smaller teams to recommend new ways to do things.

When campus leaders ask me to visit, it is usually to help staff at all levels recognize that the difficulties they are facing with budget cuts or shifting student demands are not unique to their campus. It is important to empower all staff, academic and nonacademic, to be part of the solution. Campus leaders can empower their staffs by forming task forces or working groups to identify the issues that need the most attention. The people who know each issue the best should be part of the team that makes recommendations for change. The examples in Chapter 3 are excellent in this regard. When the current student advising services do not change students' success rates or decrease time to degree, advisors have to partner with technology experts to design changes that do help students achieve their goals.

Those of you in public institutions may be interested in a recent conversation I had with Bruce Hamlett, the chief consultant for the

California State Assembly Committee on Higher Education. Bruce, who now works in California, once worked with legislators in another state and continues to monitor federal legislation on higher education. When I asked him how he imagines the future relationship between legislatures and the public higher education community, he said that he thinks states are eventually going to have problems funding higher education at the current levels. State budget pressures are growing, and higher education funding may have to be constrained—which means more costs may have to shift to students. Bruce suggested that institutions might improve their relationships with legislators if they discussed technology and other investments in the context of serving students, improving learning, and promoting efficient operations within higher education. In Chapter 5, there is an example of how California State University has tried to do just that.

A report issued by the National Center for Public Policy and Higher Education (Jones, 2006) confirms Bruce Hamlett's projection. In the national center's analysis of future state and local deficits, all states were projected to have a budget deficit by 2013. In just seven years, the center predicts deficits ranging from -0.5% to -12.9%, with a U.S. average of -5.7%. All of us know that state budget cuts are unlikely to come from primary and secondary education, corrections, or health care. Higher education will probably have to absorb most of the reductions in spending.

When you start thinking about technology as something that can help your campus become more efficient, or serve students better, try to remember something a veteran of this change process, Tad Perry, once shared with me: "The capacity to resist change is greater than the resources to implement it." In the late 1990s Tad—now the executive director of the South Dakota Board of Regents—realized that the resources in South Dakota were not enough to allow institutions to do whatever they wanted when they created online course materials. There were too few resources to fund multiple institutions to create basically the same online course over and over again. As Tad worked to ensure greater coherence and the efficient use of technology, he learned several lessons:

- Strong central leadership is necessary to wrangle all the constituent groups who will be affected by the changes.

- It is important to give the designated leader the proper resources, as it is very easy to burn that person out.

- A designated leader must have an understanding of the technical realities and academic issues involved in the process.

- It is important to have a thorough plan for the period of change. Different groups should always remain in sync with one another.

Although Tad was coordinating several institutions' use of technology, the lessons he learned apply at the campus level as well. The one thing we all hope you gain by reading this book is an awareness that it is never too early to start considering different uses for technology.

Where Things May Be Headed

As you are no doubt aware, students increasingly use mobile devices. Few students are without their cell phones or other mobile electronic tools, such as Blackberries or Trios. My colleague Ellen Wagner left formal higher education almost a decade ago to work with the development of teaching and learning materials and strategies in industry, and now heads the Worldwide Education Solutions division of Adobe Systems. She pays close attention to new trends as part of her job. Here, she addresses the use of mobile electronic devices as teaching tools.

....

Effects of Mobile Devices on Education
Ellen Wagner

Our current models for teaching and training are based on a "command and control" model (one which places an instructor in charge and establishes goals and criteria), rather than a model of communication and collaboration. As mobile device adoption continues to grow and bring new voices to the global conversation, new learning imperatives will need to be built on a foundation of constructs and practices that enable:

*   Connectedness

*   Communication

*   Creative expression

*   Collaboration

*   Cultural awareness

*   Competitiveness

The open exchange of ideas is an essential component of social learning and communications-based models of learning and performance improvement, particularly when one is dealing with cognitive performances that address abstract ideas, problem-solving, and critical thinking activities. The natural extension of open, participative communication comes as greater value is attributed to collaborative work. The establishment of collaborative frameworks will help a learning organization better execute shared visions, strategies, and tactics. People who are better connected, better informed, and better able to respond quickly to new and emerging challenges will be among the winners in this new era of ubiquitous, pervasive connectivity. (For more information see Wagner & Wilson, 2005.)

Ellen Wagner is senior director of Worldwide eLearning Solutions, Adobe Systems, Inc.

Ellen's essay echoes the things we have said throughout this book, but she brings up another important concept: equality. As I interpret these ideas for colleges and universities, it means shifting the power bases within our institutions. To create a more efficient organization, all staff members must be considered as equal players within the institutional team. We can no longer afford to have a hierarchical structure (based on command and control) in the classroom, among the faculty as producers of teaching materials and supervisors of student learning, among campus administrators, or among providers of nonacademic support services. Instead, we need to approach planning for the future of our institutions with an equality of the participants in mind—even though that is not the way that things have usually worked. Empowering those who do not consider themselves to be respected professionals is a real challenge. However, once accomplished, the ensuing burst of creativity and mutual respect will change the way people think about how they do the business of educating future generations of world citizens.

2020: Envisioning the Future Academic Ecosystem
John Witherspoon

2020: Some Global Fundamentals
Consider the world in which we live. What are some familiar 2020 characteristics that would be seen as fundamental by someone transplanted from 2005? Here's a possible list:

- Thomas Friedman's (2005) observations about a flat world resonate even more strongly in 2020. Recall that he spoke of "a playing field that allows for multiple forms of collaboration—the sharing of knowledge and work—in real time, without regard to

geography, distance, or, in the near future, even language"
(p.176).

- In 2020 real-time worldwide broadband wireless communication instantly connects people and institutions nearly everywhere. This is recognized as a key economic and social facilitator, and for those late-blooming "least developed" countries not
  yet fully connected, catching up is an urgent goal.

- This worldwide system embraces the full range of media (computation, text, audio, and visual). It provides instant language
  translation and is compatible with a growing number of user
  devices.

- Terms like *outsourcing*—so familiar in 2005—are no longer
  heard. People who develop a product, service, or process have
  most of the world instantly and routinely available as a source,
  workplace, and market.

- The near-universal availability of communication and information has extreme implications, both positive and negative. It has
  had important—even revolutionary—implications for education, and has played an equally revolutionary, but more prob-
  lematic, role in world politics. The ill-fated Nuclear Non-
  Proliferation Treaty, for example, was one casualty of easy information access. The age of the superpower appears to be over.

- Certain individuals and countries may desire isolation, but it is
  no longer feasible. Maintaining individual privacy is also
  increasingly difficult.

2020: The Academic Ecosystem

Colleges and universities in 2020 have been profoundly influenced
by an evolution in public policy. Over the past few years, our government has begun to take seriously the connection between educa-

tion and national prosperity. It knows that if a country is to be globally competitive, it must have a workforce that understands and takes a leading role in modern-day technology, manufacturing, agriculture, business practices, and productivity. All of these elements must be grounded in an understanding of the world's cultures.

Thanks to these requirements—and to the speed with which things have changed over the past few years—higher education has truly become a career-long process.

The policy emphasis on education is matched by a national focus on research and development, and there is increased liaison (even partnership) between industry and academia. The roots of this liaison have been evident over the past few decades.

Institutions, Pedagogy, and Students

What was once called distance education or e-learning now forms the core of institutions' approach to teaching and learning. This rapid evolution has been the result of:

- A career-long (perhaps lifelong) requirement to keep learning

 - The related desire of students for a "cafeteria-style" education centered around career or personal requirements rather than a specific degree or certificate

- Increased mobility of the workforce, individually and geographically

- Worldwide access to needed technologies

- Advances in technology-based pedagogy

- Advanced user identification and encryption techniques that ensure the integrity of all who use this technology

The rapid advance of technology-based teaching and learning has caused something of a revolution in several areas of higher education. For example:

- While the college or university campus outwardly looks much the same as it did a couple of decades ago, the organization of its space takes into account the sharply reduced need for traditional classrooms. Many classrooms have been reassigned for more appropriate use, and plans for campus expansion have been modified or scaled back. The earlier connection between an institution's number of classrooms and its number of students is no longer pertinent. Instead of focusing on classroom-based instruction, the campus is headquarters to a borderless education service/enterprise.

- The campus's role has shifted, but this is not to suggest that its traditional functions have disappeared. Generations of students have been shaped by the experience of campus life, especially the time they spent socializing with peers and being influenced by dedicated professors. In 2020 on-campus students still relish these experiences (even as they take an increasing number of their courses online). Of course, this paper deals with technology-related change, not legacies (however valuable they may be).

- There is no denying that it is a challenge to include social and personal experiences in an instructional program. Techniques may have changed, but people remain social animals. When programs and students are not tied to geography, the social limits become apparent. Communication methods of 2020 (including quality email, game interactions, and video teleconferences) are common and valuable, but this remains a difficult issue.

- An increasing number of colleges and universities have joined forces with their international peers to offer programs worldwide. In a parallel development, a new type of institution has emerged to serve this international education marketplace.

- Student services have become interactive online, providing students—regardless of location—with advising and mentoring help. Staff are able to dispense information about students' progress toward their degrees and certifications, suggest related programs for future consideration, offer course alternatives, and give them access to other students in comparable situations.

- The nature of a faculty member's job has changed dramatically, with much less emphasis on classroom-based teaching and more focus on mentoring, evaluation, and research. The number of faculty members at a traditional campus has declined significantly.

The most profound changes are taking place in the development, format, and management of courses. The growth of online courses, coupled with the advent of longer, more mobile careers, has substantially altered our educational landscape.

Consider the following progression, which reflects some current variations and some from the recent past:

- Building on earlier models pioneered by institutions such as the University of Phoenix and the University of Maryland University College, courses are not the work of an individual faculty member, but rather the product of faculty consensus, with all concerned teaching the same "standard" course.

- Moving beyond that model, groups of institutions collaborate in the design of courses to be offered online and equally accept each other's credits.

- Pedagogical entrepreneurs form companies to design, produce, and market courses.

- These courses may be licensed to conventional institutions or sold directly to students, with certificates possibly being offered upon completion.

- Instead of being focused on a degree, students are more concerned with career-based learning requirements. Institutions respond to their needs in a variety of ways (some, unfortunately, without high ethical standards).

- Courseware libraries offer courses to institutions or individuals. Some courses are formally peer evaluated; some are not.

During the past few years, it became possible—even common—for students to obtain degrees and certificates entirely online. Some were offered by accredited colleges and universities; others, by a variety of entities. Some of the latter offered rigorous, top-quality programs; others essentially sold work-free diplomas.

Overall, the number of campus-based institutions declined somewhat, while the number of higher education entities grew significantly.

How could institutions demonstrate worth amid such a profusion of products? In response to market demand, the number of accreditors (and of entities prepared to provide certificates of accreditation) multiplied. In this free-for-all, finding a way to demonstrate integrity and establish consistent standards became a matter of urgency.

Governments recognized the need for an internationally reliable certification of quality. After long debate, the U.S. government, in concert with the governments of many other concerned nations, declared that any institution that offers degrees or certificates must be accredited by an independent organization that meets specific academic standards. In addition, considering the multiplicity of sources for the courses now offered by these programs, it was soon determined that classes must be peer reviewed for their rigor and validity of content.

There was, of course, an instant outcry about the value of market forces, entrepreneurial spirit, and independent student judgment. To date, however, formal accreditation prevails. Currently pending is a requirement that peer review be extended to those offering certificates of completion for individual courses.

Over the years, there has been a significant evolution in the techniques used in the courses and the ways in which student achievement is evaluated. Some key elements are:

- Courses may periodically engage groups of students in working together or competing against one another. Learning techniques have been adapted from wildly popular online games. As in those games, participants may be anywhere.

- As previously noted, peer-evaluated courses are now produced independently by many institutions or individuals. From this ever-growing base, entities that offer related degrees or certificates may license and offer those courses that they deem appropriate. Since courses are self-contained and come with a guarantee of quality, the transfer of credits between institutions is much easier.

- Institutions of higher education have almost universally adopted competence-based grading standards rather than letter grades. Techniques developed over the past decade ensure that students are objectively evaluated against a mastery-of-content baseline. At the end of a course, there should be no question of whether someone truly understands the material and can apply it properly and reliably.

Summary

The academic ecosystem of 2020 is a major element of our flat world, shaped by the social and economic changes spawned by modern technology. Through education and research, it also shapes the course of change and the leveling of the global playing field.

Higher education, once designed to offer advanced learning to the elite, has become a core requirement in 2020's global society. As education's mission has changed, so have its methodology and organization. The traditional rural campus has become a multilayered international enterprise for learning and research. The typical course is designed, produced, offered, and taken electronically, with continuous support from faculty, mentors, and peers. There is quality control in accreditation for the institution, peer review for the course, and objective competency measures for the student.

For students—as for most of today's citizens—the need for education has become increasingly urgent. The need exists throughout one's whole career, if not one's life. As a result, higher education must be available wherever and whenever it is needed. Students' support network (the institution and its other students) may vary with time and geography, but there will always be a need for consistent quality and availability.

Higher education in 2020 is part of a new world. The challenges, demands, and rewards have no precedent—and no boundaries.

Author's note: An earlier version of this essay appears on the WECT web site (www.wcet.info).

John P. Witherspoon, a WCET senior advisor, is one of the visionary leaders who helped establish WCET in 1989. He is also professor emeritus of San Diego State University and has worked with WCET on assignments too numerous to mention.

John Witherspoon's essay really does sum it all up. \
that this is where we are headed within the next decad‹
will be a challenge, but it is a challenge we must face if
we care about are to thrive. We all know we have to be more efficient,
and there is no doubt in my mind that the wise use of new technology
will be an important part of achieving that efficiency.

I hope that some of the strategies touched on in this book will be of
value as you begin your journey toward institutional transformation.
Much is possible, but transformation will require doing things differently. It will require engaging the entire campus community in thinking
about what each member has to offer. It will require academic and
administrative leaders to rethink current policies that impede change. It
will require governing board members, as well as legislators, to support
campus leaders in what seem like radical changes. But it can be done!

Endnote

1) This information comes from a conversation I had with
   Smarthinking's CEO, Burck Smith, in early 2006.

References

Carson, S. (2006). *2005 Program evaluation findings report: MIT OpenCourseWare*. Cambridge, MA: Massachusetts Institute of Technology.

Friedman, T. L. (2005). *The world is flat: A brief history of the twenty-first century*. New York, NY: Farrar, Straus, and Giroux.

Jones, D. (2006, February). State shortfalls projected despite economic gains: Long-term prospects for higher education no brighter. *Policy Alert.* The National Center for Public Policy and Higher Education.

Open University. (2006). *Open content initiative.* Retrieved on July 18, 2006, from: http://oci.open.ac.uk/

Remember Detroit. (2006, March 11). *The Economist,* p. 11.

Wagner, E. D., & Wilson, P. R. (2005, December). Disconnected. *T&D Magazine, 59*(12), 40–43.

··· Index